60 0059035 9
KU-515-836

Problems of urban passenger transport

CLIFFORD SHARP

Problems of urban passenger transport

with special reference to Leicester

LEICESTER UNIVERSITY PRESS
1967

Printed in Great Britain
by C. H. Gee & Co. Ltd., Leicester,
for the Leicester University Press
SBN 7185 1074 7

PREFACE

This study of some of the problems of passenger transport in Britain today has been based in part on a survey of passenger transport in the Leicester area made for the East Midlands Economic Planning Council and the Ministry of Transport. The terms of reference of the original study were 'to study and report on passenger transport in the Leicester area with a view to establishing what improvements, if any, might be made in the present pattern in order to make the most efficient and economic use of the available resources and to examine ways and means of making these more attractive to the travelling public.' In this book the Leicester case study has been used to illustrate and discuss the problems of urban passenger transport found in the country as a whole.

In carrying out the Leicester survey I had the benefit of the help of a Working Group in collecting and interpreting information, and reported to a Steering Group whose criticisms and opinions were extremely valuable. The opinions expressed in the original report, and in this book, are, however, my own. Mr L. H. Smith and Mr D. R. Smith of Leicester City Transport, and Mr D. Fytche and Mr J. Isaac of the Birmingham and Midland Motor Omnibus Co. (which for convenience I have called by its more popular name of 'Midland Red' in the rest of this book) were particularly generous in allowing me to take up their time when I was seeking advice and information. Both bus undertakings provided me with most valuable information on their operations for which I am grateful. There are some points made in this book with which the bus undertakings would not agree, and, in particular, the Midland Red representatives feel that my suggestion that a single undertaking should operate all the bus services in Leicester and Leicestershire is not justified. Mr E. Mycock of British Rail provided me with most useful data on rail services in the Leicester area.

I must also acknowledge the help and information which I received from members of the City Engineer's and City Planning Officer's Departments and from Mr Sheridan, the East Midlands Traffic Commissioner. My assistant Mr K. Usher received considerable help from Mr Jones of the Midland Red and from Mr Gillam of the City Engineer's Department. Mr Topham of the D.E.A. has helped me with problems connected with the presentation of the original report, and Mr Farnsworth, chairman of the East Midlands Economic Planning Board, gave me general guidance and help during the carrying out of the research. Professor R. L. Meek of the University of Leicester, who acted as chairman of the Steering Group, also helped me considerably in discussing the analysis and presentation of the results of the survey.

Finally I must acknowledge the very intensive work both on the research project and on this book, which has been carried out by my research assistant Mr K. Usher, by my secretary/research assistant Miss M. Jewsbury, and by my former secretary, Mrs D. Spathaky.

Leicester, 1967 CLIFFORD SHARP

CONTENTS

TEXT FIGURES

TABLES

1

General survey of the problems of urban passenger transport

That transport in towns is a major problem of life in Britain today is self-evident. The symptoms of an over-strained transport system can be experienced in the daily lives of almost all of us. Noise, exhaust fumes and the delays and dangers of crossing the street; very slow travel by car through congested streets and the long search for a parking space; irregular and overcrowded rush-hour bus services and the spoliation by traffic of once-attractive town centres – all these are now part of everyday life in Britain. The symptoms are obvious; but diagnosis and cure is another matter. The problems of congestion are so common in the world today, and so apparently deep-rooted that few people can still believe in any easy or obvious solution.

There are three main components of the growth of traffic on urban roads which has taken place in recent years; an increased demand for personal travel into and through city centre areas; a growth in the number of goods vehicles on the roads; and a transfer of passengers from public transport to private car. In attempting to analyse the problem of congestion and consider possible remedies it is important to distinguish between the main sources of the growth of passenger traffic. Measures aimed at stabilizing or reducing the number of people working in city centre areas are unlikely to have any effect on the choice between bus, train and private car as a means of transport. It is clearly important to have some estimate of the relative importance of changes both in the demand for urban transport and in the 'modal split' between different forms of passenger transport on the future demand for road space. Policies concerned with the choice between public and private transport, with which this study will be mainly concerned, may be effective in a relatively short run period; those relating to total travel demand will be long term, and involve important issues relating to town planning and industrial location, as well as considerations of transport economics and traffic engineering.

The problems of transport in towns today are the product of a number of complex technological, social and economic changes. They are the result of technological advances, side by side with technological obsolescence; they are linked with profound changes in the social class structure and chosen way of life of people in Britain, and reflect complicated movements in the location of business and industry. The industrial towns of the nineteenth century were built on the basic assumption that people would walk to work. In the smaller towns it was also possible to walk into the shopping area of the town centre. The larger towns were really groups of industrial villages, each 'village' being a largely self-contained community with its own factories, shops and houses all situated very near to each other. These larger towns may also have had central areas (though some, like Stoke-on-Trent, still retain the pattern of a number of individual towns which have met at the edges), but the bulk of the population only travelled into these occasionally, and then by foot or by horse-drawn public transport. There were suburbs in the larger cities for the relatively wealthy, but the distance of these from the central area was generally limited by the speed of horse-drawn transport. Some more outlying residential suburbs developed around railway lines towards the end of the nineteenth century, but again, these were very much for a minority of middle-class people. Bulk movement of passenger traffic is a twentieth-century phenomenon brought about by the development of suburban rail services, electric tramways, the motor bus, the underground and, most important of all, the motor car. Once it became economically and technologically possible to live some way from one's work and yet reach it in a reasonable time, a large demand to move away from central city areas developed. This outward movement of population, together with a continual growth of large urban areas, and the development of new complex travel patterns, has resulted in what is really a whole series of transport problems. Although there has been considerable technical advance in the development of buses, cars and electric rail transport, there is still very considerable obsolescence in the provision of road track. Many roads, particularly near the centre of the larger cities, remain as they were in the nineteenth century, when they were designed for purely local traffic only, and the great volume of traffic now coming in from the outer suburbs was not envisaged.

There is no doubt that total demand for passenger transport in Britain has been increasing continuously in recent years. Table 1 shows the estimated total passenger flows in Britain from 1955–65, and their division between the different transport modes.

Table 1. Estimated total passenger transport in Great Britain[1] ('000 million passenger miles)

Year	Air	Rail	Public road transport	Private road transport	Total
1955	0.2	23.8	49.8	54.3	128.1
1956	0.3	24.5	48.6	59.5	132.9
1957	0.3	25.9	45.9	59.9	132.0
1958	0.3	25.5	43.4	72.9	142.1
1959	0.4	25.5	44.1	82.1	152.1
1960	0.5	24.8	43.9	88.9	158.1
1961	0.6	24.1	43.1	97.7	165.5
1962	0.7	22.8	42.4	103.7	169.6
1963	0.8	22.4	41.5	110.5	175.2
1964	0.9	23.0	40.3	125.5	189.7
1965	1.0	21.8	37.6	134.8	195.2

[1] *Passenger Transport in Great Britain*, 1965. Table I, p. 2.

Thus there has been an increase of 52.4% in total passenger mileage in the ten-year period. But these figures do not show how much of this increase relates to travel in urban areas, and unfortunately there are no national figures separating out urban and rural demand over a period of time on a comparable basis. It is possible, however, to make some guesses about what has happened, or is likely to happen, to passenger flows in urban areas by analysing some of the factors influencing demand. In this context, 'urban areas' may be restricted to towns and conurbations with populations of at least 100,000 people. Any dividing line in this context is clearly arbitrary, but this figure fits in with that used by the American International Urban Research team, who defined an 'urban unit' as a place '. . . containing a population of at least 100,000 people, being an area embracing a central city or cities, plus adjacent areas with an economic relationship with that city and with 65% or more of economically-active populations engaged in non-agricultural activities.'* This definition would probably include several towns in Britain where the central town has a population of less than 100,000, though the phrase 'an economic relationship' allows for considerable variations in interpretation. The most important transport factor which empirical evidence has shown to be related to size is that the proportion of through traffic generally decreased with increasing size.† This study will be concerned with towns where the main transport problem does not come from through traffic.

One of the chief determinants of the demand for travel into city centre

* Peter Hall, *The World Cities*, p. 19.

† See *Urban Traffic Engineering Techniques*, H.M.S.O., pp. 6–7.

areas is the number of jobs available there. To predict what will happen to the total number of job opportunities in urban areas in the future is a complex study in itself.

In Britain the government has made some efforts to limit the development of new offices in the centre of London, and other large cities. The Location of Offices Bureau was set up in April 1963 to persuade offices to move from central London to other places, and particularly to those areas with above average rates of unemployment. In the three years from 1963–66 318 firms, with 30,251 job opportunities, moved from central London, though 163 of these did not go outside Greater London. In 1966/67 the bureau succeeded in moving a further 11,718 jobs out of London.* The Industrial Development Act of 1965 gave power to the government to control office development by licensing, and these powers have been applied widely in the midlands and the south. Although there are no really adequate figures of employment in central London, there is some evidence that total employment may now no longer be increasing, and may even be decreasing. The insurance cards exchanged at central London exchanges (City, Westminster, West End, Holborn and Borough) reached a peak of 1,646,000 in 1963, having increased each year since 1952 when the figure was 1,378,000, but these figures fell to 1,634,000 in 1964 and 1,528,000 in 1965.† There are various statistical problems in interpreting these figures, such as the exclusion of most civil servants, and the practice of some firms of exchanging cards from central London headquarters offices for employees who work elsewhere, but it would be very surprising if they were not highly correlated with the true employment trends. London Transport's estimates of total passenger traffic into central London between 7 and 10 A.M. suggests fluctuations in recent years, but no upward trend. Thus figures for the years 1960 to 1965 were (in thousands) 1,192, 1,213, 1,238, 1,196, 1,200 and 1,183 respectively.‡

For manufacturing industry there has been a movement away from city centre areas which is likely to continue. Most modern production processes demand plant layouts which are only suitable for single storey buildings, and the cost of land in central areas makes expansion there impracticable. There are some exceptions to this, such as the Birmingham jewellery industry, which can be housed in 'flatted factories,' but generally the number of jobs in

* Location of Offices Bureau *Annual Reports*, 1965–66, 1966–67.

† A. W. Evans, 'Myths about Employment in Central London,' *Journal of Transport Economics and Policy*, May 1967, p. 218.

‡ A. W. Evans, *op. cit.*, p. 217.

manufacturing industry in city central areas is likely to continue to decline.

To some extent the demand for transport into central areas and the provision of transport facilities are interdependent. Increasing congestion and parking difficulties can lead to the siting of both offices and shops in outer suburban areas. The motor car, which is the main cause of city centre congestion, also in part provides a remedy, since it makes the suburban location of offices and large shops possible. One of the traditional reasons for siting offices in city centres has been the need to have the offices where they could easily be reached by public transport for the benefit of the many women clerical workers who could not afford a car. As more and more people are able to buy cars so this constraint becomes less important.

Some important figures for 39 major American cities (excluding New York) are given by Meyer, Kain and Wohl in their recent book on urban transportation,* and these are reproduced in Table 2.

Table 2. Average annual percentage changes in population and employment, 39 American cities, adjusted for boundary alterations[1]

Item	Central city			Suburban ring		
	'48–'54	'54–'58	'48–'58	'48–'54	'54–'58	'48–'58
Manufacturing	1.9	–1.7	–0.6	13.2	7.0	15.0
Wholesaling	0.9	0.2	0.7	25.4	16.8	29.4
Retailing	–0.6	0.1	–0.4	11.5	13.6	16.0
Services	1.6	3.9	2.7	18.2	16.8	24.4
Population	0.2	0.1	0.2	8.8	6.4	9.4

[1]Meyer, Kain and Wohl, *The Urban Transportation Problem*, Table 2, p. 28.

The job opportunities in these American central city areas grew very much less than those in the 'suburban rings,' and employment in manufacturing and in retailing declined. Very much the same situation may be expected in British cities, although the development of suburban shopping centres is less advanced in Britain than in the United States.

The second major factor influencing the demand for travel into central city areas is where people choose to live. The decision where to live can be the result of a complicated 'trade-off' between housing costs, the cost of travelling to work, and the relative pleasantness of different areas of residence. Based mainly on an empirical study of travel in Chicago and Detroit, Meyer, Kain and Wohl concluded that 'American urban households apparently have a choice between spending more for transportation and less for housing (quality

* Meyer, Kain and Wohl, *The Urban Transportation Problem*, Harvard University Press, 1965.

held constant), or the reverse.*

The relationship between housing and transport costs in a city depends upon a rather complicated set of interdependent factors. If everyone worked in the city centre and the journey to work was their only transport cost, if transport costs were a function only of distance, and if all areas were equally attractive for housing, then the price of the same quality of house would tend to decrease with distance from the city centre as transport costs increased. But none of these assumptions holds in the real world. The transport costs of shopping, schooling and recreation must be considered as well as that of the work journeys. The relationship between work and other transport costs will vary from town to town and suburb to suburb, and also with the tastes of individual families. If the quality of the house (and garden) is held constant then the main factor affecting cost will be the price of land. But the demand for land comes not only from potential house owners but also from many industrial and commercial users for whom the costs of passenger travel to the city centre are unimportant. There may also be many people seeking houses in a suburb who do not work in the city centre, but whose demand will affect land prices. There is also another most important variable, besides land and building costs, which affects housing prices. This may be called 'amenity' and includes all quality factors apart from that of the actual house and garden itself, and apart from transport considerations. The most important of these would be environment, the nature of the other development in the area. Thus plots of building land of half an acre in an inner suburb and an outer suburb might both be on sale at the same price but the outer suburban plot be preferred by the typical city centre worker, despite lower transport costs from the inner suburb, because of the greatly superior amenity value of the outer suburb. To make the analysis even more realistic the 'residential' demand for land could be subdivided according to the density of development which would-be purchasers are prepared to accept. The cost of land in the inner suburb may be as high as that in the outer suburb because of a greater demand for high density and for non-residential development there. But city centre workers may be predominantly those whose preference is for low-density, high amenity housing. These factors will completely swamp the low travel cost advantages of the inner suburbs, which may well become inhabited by people working in middle or outer ring industrial plants.

As income levels rise so people tend to move out to lower density outer suburbs while other families formerly not having their own homes at all occupy

* Meyer, Kain and Wohl, *op. cit.*, p. 142.

the high density inner suburban accommodation. The way in which many British cities have developed may result in a somewhat irrational location of population in relation to transport facilities and their place of work. City centre workers with income levels leading them to demand high quality, low density housing are forced to travel to the outer suburbs while inner suburbs may be occupied by industrial workers whose journey to work takes them further out to outer ring factories. It is only where the inner suburb is composed of decayed high quality housing that it can be rehabilitated piecemeal. The typical nineteenth-century mixed industrial and residential inner suburb would need to be comprehensively redeveloped to raise its amenity standards sufficiently for it to provide a real alternative as a place to live for those now commuting from the outer suburbs. Thus a city centre worker in Birmingham seeking low density, high amenity housing (but not able to afford the price of such accommodation in the inner suburb of Edgbaston), would find that, on the northeastern side of the city, he would probably have to travel as far as Sutton Coldfield to obtain what he wanted. Low density housing does not exist in the intervening inner suburb of Aston or (except on the fringe of Sutton) in the 'middle-ring' suburb of Erdington. People living in Aston probably work mainly in local industry or travel away from central Birmingham to the industrial concentrations at Witton and Tyburn.

The interrelationship between housing and transport costs, and the choice of where to live is further complicated in that the cost of transport must be met in the 'double currency' of both money and time.* It seems likely that the time costs of travelling may generally be more important than the money costs in influencing land prices, and the decision on where to live. Time and money travelling costs are interchangeable in so far as a more extensive and quicker form of transport can be substituted for a slower and cheaper form and to the extent that housing nearer to the central business district can be bought instead of that which is further away. Since there is relatively little scope for the former substitution and since the marginal utility of leisure will generally increase very rapidly when the total working day, including travelling time, rises above about ten hours, the cost of land may be expected to fall quite rapidly (other things being equal) when it is more than about an hour's journey from the city centre. In smaller towns this fall in land values would come more quickly. In the Leicester area, for example, there is still a fairly plentiful supply of potential building land which is no more than thirty

* Consumer behaviour under 'double currency' conditions is discussed in Lowdon Wingo, Jr., *Transportation and Urban Land*, p. 53 *et seq.*

minutes' journey from the city centre by car, and land prices would not, therefore, be expected to fall much more for land still further out, though this can, of course, be affected by changes in the designation of 'Green Belt' land. Travelling times do not vary directly with distance but are dependent on the nature of the roads and the public transport facilities. In the larger towns with considerable traffic congestion problems commuter rail lines usually provide the quickest form of transport to the city centre, and there is likely to be a clear relationship between land and housing values and nearness to a commuter station. The work journey to the city centre from some inner suburbs with no commuter train stations may be as long or longer than that from more outlying residential areas.

The money costs of transport to work may also become significantly large when it becomes necessary to use private rather than public transport. The first 'cost barrier' which must be broken through is that of the purchase of a car. But once a car is owned most people consider only the marginal cost of its use on work trips, arguing (if they rationalize their behaviour) that they must have the car for pleasure purposes and that the maintenance and depreciation costs need not be charged against the work journey. On this basis, charging only fuel costs and perhaps some 'wear and tear' to the journey to work, the cost of one person using a car is roughly the same as the level of bus fares. With one passenger the car will, on this basis of comparison, generally be cheaper than any form of public transport. It is only when high parking charges must be paid that travelling to work by car becomes obviously more expensive than public transport. In the centres of the largest cities like London the ability to use a private car may depend on status, the right to use one of a limited number of parking spaces owned by the firm or department, rather than wealth alone.

The relative importance of the effect of money and time travelling costs on land prices can be illustrated by simple examples. The current cost of a rail three-monthly season ticket from Sutton Coldfield to Birmingham is £10. Assuming the payment of a net interest rate of 5% on borrowed capital, this would mean that a house from which it was possible to walk to work in central Birmingham which was identical in 'amenity' with one in Sutton would have £800 added to its value to reflect travelling money cost differences. But if it is assumed that the total daily door to door travelling time between Sutton Coldfield and an office in central Birmingham was one hour longer than that from an equivalent house in an inner suburb, that the total working year contains 240 days, and that the marginal value of leisure for potential commuters is 10*s*. an hour, then this would represent an annual cost of £120, or a capital sum of £2400 (with a 5% net interest rate). Thus the total cost differential between houses of identical amenity in Sutton and inner Birmingham for city central workers would be £3200. This does not of course mean that this is the actual price differential one would expect to find even if the assumptions were true, as there are other demands for land and housing besides those of city centre workers, but it does imply that such a worker would pay up to £3200 more for a house with the travelling characteristics of inner Birmingham compared with those of Sutton Coldfield, all other things being the same. A similar London example would be the journey from Bromley South to Victoria which costs £13 10*s*. per quarter, the yield of a capital sum of £1080 at 5%. These figures suggest that about one quarter of the 'cost differential' between equivalent central and urban housing reflects money travelling costs, and three quarters time travelling costs. But the marginal value of leisure, which will be closely associated with income, may be much higher than 10*s*. an hour and it would not be difficult to explain even the very high prices of high amenity housing near central London largely in terms of the time costs of travelling.

Even this brief analysis of the complex issues involved may show how difficult it is to generalize about the total demand for transport into the centre of cities. Future changes in the number of people employed in city centre areas are uncertain, and will vary from city to city. As has already been argued, there is some evidence that in the largest conurbations like London employment figures may have reached a 'plateau.' The day of the ultimate traffic jam may not come so inevitably as a simple projection of recent trends in car ownership and the move from public to private transport might suggest because of the interdependence of travelling conditions and demand. Travel for non-work purposes is even more difficult to predict. While the central areas of the great metropolitan cities of the world will no doubt continue to attract people for shopping and entertainment, other towns may develop large scale suburban shopping centres on the American pattern and thus reduce the demand for city centre shopping. The new Woolco department store in the Oadby residential suburb of Leicester is planned to draw shoppers out from inner Leicester as well as serving its immediate neighbourhood and the country beyond. The movement of population seems likely to follow its present trend away from the inner suburbs (and indeed out of the outer suburbs of yesterday) for some years to come. But there are obviously limits to the outward movement of people who must work in the city centre. Unless some new method of rapid urban transport is developed or large scale investment in new electric rail lines and urban motorways is allowed, it seems unlikely that the London 'commuter country' will spread out to very much greater distances than it does at present, though there are some gaps in the existing rings of development which could be filled. In a paper read at a Ministry of Transport 'Open Day' in April 1967, Mr D. T. Cairns, of British Rail, argued that there is still 'a measure of net advantage to be gained by long distance commuters in respect of the trade off between house prices and rail fares' and that therefore a continued expansion of the commuting area might be expected. But this argument appears to measure only the money cost of travelling and exclude the time costs which, as has been shown above, may be much more important. If a continued expansion of the London commuter belt were to be encouraged, this would probably involve building new electric rail lines with stations planned with really large scale car parks. Although fast electric trains may make journeys of 50 miles or more in an hour the problem of congestion and slow travel on the last leg of the homeward journey may just be moved out to the area around the distant station. Thus it is possible to travel from London to Brighton in an hour but the total work journey of anyone living in a suburb of Brighton could be much longer. There are two developments which could affect the expansion of commuter country. Inner suburbs might become much more pleasant places in which city centre workers would be content to live. This could be the result of the rehabilitation of former residential areas which have decayed with the outward movement of population but which might become attractive again with increasing travel difficulties from the outer suburbs. It is also possible that some of the dreary high density inner suburbs, built in Victorian times for workers in nearby industry, could be rebuilt as pleasant residential areas. Secondly the growth of new towns which provide both work and homes for people can greatly reduce the demand for travel into central city areas. This development can lead to some confusion in that these new towns may be within the boundaries of the larger 'city-regions,' and census figures may show an outward movement of population which is not a 'commuter' development. Thus the population of the London city region as defined by the standards of the International Urban Research team mentioned above, was 11,547,000 in 1961*. But this figure includes Stevenage, Welwyn, Hatfield, Harlow, Basildon, Crawley, Bracknell and Hemel Hempstead new towns part of whose *raison d'etre* is to prevent surburban sprawl and the further growth of 'dormitory' towns for

* P. Hall, *The World Cities*, p. 23.

commuters. (Although there is some evidence that the new towns may be providing more commuters to central London than was intended.) Since urban developments of the size of London and New York exist and their transport systems do function, however inefficiently, it is obvious that much smaller cities like Leicester could still expand very greatly.

The size of the future demand for passenger transport will be determined, it appears, by a number of interdependent factors. To a very considerable extent demand can be expected to expand to use up whatever extra transport facilities are provided. New investment in surface and underground railway lines, in urban motorways, and in new forms of transport like monorails and elevated bus tracks, will lead to strong pressure for the further growth of large cities. Conversely, failure to make new investments to improve roads or to provide extra parking places means that transport facilities will act as a major constraint preventing further urban growth. In recent years urban growth has taken place at the cost of overburdening transport facilities with a consequent decline in quality. But, as has now been widely recognized, there are limits to this process and increased pressure on road transport in many cities could lead to complete breakdown. The main message of the Buchanan Report *Traffic in Towns* was that to meet the demand for motor traffic which would result from allowing recent trends to continue into the early years of the twenty-first century would involve the complete rebuilding of city centres, with very large scale investment. This level of investment is almost certainly greater than the country could afford, and in any case, it is very doubtful whether the type of city which would result, with sixteen- or twenty-lane motorways converging on the central area, would be the kind of place people want to live in. There are, therefore, in the long run, important decisions about the kind of urban development which should be planned for the future and transport investments decisions must be related to the planned maximum size of towns and to the development of the kind of environment in which people wish to live, work and play.

A very important part of the whole problem of urban congestion is to find the right level of investment in new roads and in road improvements; in cars, buses and rail passenger locomotives and carriages; in new tube rail lines and extensions; and in possible new forms of urban transportation such as monorails and elevated bus roads. To find the optimum level of investment in urban transport involves first of all deciding the total level of investment for the country over a period of years, then on the proper allocation for transport, then on the allocation between urban and rural (or inter-urban) transport, then in each sector between road and rail, and finally between a large number of possible road alternatives. Investment policy in the end depends upon value judgments in comparing potential improvements in the welfare of different sections of the community, using estimates of costs and benefits which must both be subject to very considerable uncertainties. The total sum allocated to public transport investment in Britain (mainly investment in the railways, in the Transport Holding Company's undertakings and in road track) is decided as a result of bargaining in the Treasury and the Cabinet and the interaction of different pressure groups in presenting their demands to the government. Even the allocation between road and rail is determined not through any centralized economic planning but, as far as can be gathered from the outside, by similar interacting pressures applied to the Treasury and the Cabinet by the Ministry of Transport (mainly in its road providing capacity), British Railways Board, and to a much smaller extent by bodies such as the British Road Federation and the (pro-rail) National Council for Inland Transport. A Highway Economics Unit has recently been set up in the Ministry of Transport to plan for the best use of £200 million or so which is now spent annually on inter-urban highways. This will produce a report in October 1967 dealing with the basic economic theory of cost-benefit analysis. It is evident that, if the machinery for a rational choice between alternative inter-urban road investments has only just been formed, many other higher level investment decisions may have been taken without adequate examination. Investment in road vehicles is of course the result of countless individual decisions (which can, however, be influenced by the government through its tax policies and control of hire purchase regulations). It would be very surprising if the sum finally allocated to the improvement of urban passenger transport facilities was in any sense optimal but to determine what that optimum ought to be is beyond the scope of the present study. As already argued, the size of the optimum investment in urban passenger transport depends upon value judgments and some guesswork about the desired pattern of urban life in the twenty-first century as well as measuring the costs and benefits of alternative investment in such projects as hospitals, roads and nuclear power stations. In the main the problems of urban passenger transport in this study will be discussed within the framework of the existing investment policy. This does not imply any kind of justification for existing policy and, in particular, the question of whether very much larger sums should not be allocated to urban road improvement is left open. To argue that some transport and planning problems would remain even with the most massive new investment does not mean that investment ought not to increase. Often-quoted American experience shows that private transport alone is inadequate for passenger transport in large cities; it does not show that Britain ought not to spend a great deal more money than at present on improving urban roads.

Given the very limited levels of current investment in urban transport, the considerable overstraining of existing road facilities, and at least the maintenance of existing total levels of demand to make journeys on urban roads, the problem becomes one of making the best possible use of the transport resources now available.

The basic scarce resource, the supply of which cannot easily be increased in cities, is land for road and rail track and to provide parking space for cars, buses, lorries, locomotives, rail carriages and aeroplanes. The principal theme of this study, and the main hope of improving urban transportation without massive investment or completely redesigning our towns, are found in the fact that some forms of transport make a more economical use of road space than others. There is widespread agreement today amongst those who have studied urban transport problems (though not necessarily amongst travellers) that a greater use must be made of public transport in towns. Thus at the Second International Conference on Urban Transportation held in Pittsburgh in April 1967, Dr F. Seitz, president of the U.S. National Academy of Sciences, argued that 'mass transportation is the only solution for bringing people into the cities'* and Mr L. Cusick, the Director of Urban Transportation in the U.S. Department of Housing and Urban Development, said that '. . . commuting journeys from suburbs are becoming long and tiring. This trend must be reversed by improved transportation systems which will involve less use of private cars.'† In calculations relating speed to the volume of traffic flow a bus is generally estimated to be the equivalent of three 'passenger car units' (though this figure may vary in different road conditions). With average car loads of approximately 1.5 persons on urban roads during the peak periods when congestion is most serious, this means that any bus with more than 4.5 passengers is using less road space per passenger than a private car. At this level of loading buses would almost certainly have lower overall efficiency than cars when the cost of the other scarce resources of labour and capital equipment were considered, but at normal peak loading levels of 40–45 passengers they would easily be the lower-cost operators.

* Reported in *Transportation Bulletin*, No. 6, p. 6, U.K. Scientific Mission.
† *Ibid.*, p. 6.

Figures of passenger transport in London in 1962 show that in peak periods cars and motor cycles formed about 54.8% of the traffic flow (measured in passenger car units) compared with a figure for buses and coaches of 15.6%. But cars and motor cycles only carried 12.5% of the total commuter traffic compared with 23.0% carried by buses and coaches.* By far the most important cause of the difficulties of urban passenger transport today is that people have been increasingly choosing to travel by private car rather than by low cost buses or trains. (Though how far passenger trains do have lower overall costs is a more complex issue than that of the comparison between bus and car costs, and this is considered in more detail in Chapter 7.) There are two reasons for this. The chief and obvious reason is that transport is not a homogeneous service and that the quality of private car transport is generally regarded as being much higher than that of public transport. This is because it is instantly available, normally provides a through door to door service, does not involve walking or waiting in wet or cold weather, and is usually the quickest form of transport. Secondly, and very much less important, is the fact that the costs of alternative transport modes may not be accurately reflected in the prices charged for travel by bus and train, and in the 'prices' which car owners impute to themselves for private motoring. This point is developed in Chapter 3. If people freely choose to travel into city centre areas by private car, can there be any reasons justifying interference by the government with that free choice? The basic answer to this, which is the main theme of Chapter 5, is that although when an individual chooses between public and private transport, the private car may offer a clearly superior service, this might not be true in the case of the collective choice of a large number of travellers. The transfer of one traveller from car to bus or train would have no appreciable effect on congestion levels but the movement of whole groups of commuters certainly would do so. Dr Mishan has analysed this situation in terms of consumers' surplus. He postulates three phases of the situation when an individual decides to buy a car to be used in commuting to work. In Phase I only public transport exists, and an individual A decides to buy a car on an estimate of benefits and cost which allows for the time savings which would be possible if there were no traffic congestion. In Phase III many other people have bought cars and the time of the work journey is lengthened so that A would now be better off in Phase I, but this

* *Better Use of Town Roads*, Ministry of Transport, 1967, pp. 9–10.

situation is no longer available since public transport has now been made slower by the growth of car traffic.*

There has been a clear and continued swing away from the use of public passenger transport in recent years. As the figures in Table 1 show, while total estimated passenger mileage in Great Britain increased by 52.4% between 1955 and 1965, rail passenger mileage decreased by 8.4% and public road transport mileage by 24.5% in the same period. In 1965 rail carried an estimated 11.2% of total passenger mileage, public service road vehicles 19.3%, and private road transport 69.0%.† Measured by passenger journeys, the passenger traffic carried by British Railways declined by 13.0% between 1955 and 1965, while the passengers carried by London Transport rail fell by 2.8%. Travel by bus stage services declined by 28.0% in the same period while the number of passenger journeys made by Express services increased by 13.4%. Out of total passenger journeys made in 1965 of 11,652 million, however, only 76 million were on Express services and 11,193 million were on stage vehicles, though if passenger mileage figures were available, Excursion services with their much higher average mileages would

Table 3. Peak year for passengers carried, 16 towns in Great Britain

Year	Town	Peak annual passenger journeys (millions)
1946	Aberdeen	69
1948	Leicester	102
1949	Southport	32
1950	Birkenhead	78
	Manchester	417
	Salford	116
	Wallasey	37
1952	Nottingham	173
	Rotherham	64
1953	Haslingden	5
1954	Bedwas and Machen	1
1956	Teesside	12
1957	Edinburgh	238
1958	Dundee	82
	South Shields	43
1959	Sunderland	87

* E. J. Mishan, 'Interpretation of the Benefits of Private Transport,' *Journal of Transport Economics and Policy*, May, 1967, pp. 184–189.

† *Passenger Transport in Great Britain*, 1965, Table 2.

be relatively a little more important.* The decline in passenger journeys on stage services in London in the 1955–65 period was 38.4% while on local authority undertakings in the main urban areas it was 25.3% and on services in 'smaller urban, semi-urban and rural areas' it was 25.7%.† The records of individual transport undertakings reveal a standard pattern of traffic reaching an annual peak and then declining continuously, from which there are few divergences. The only apparent difference of importance is that the peak year for passengers carried was much later in some towns than in others. The peak year for sixteen towns and the passengers carried in that year are shown in Table 3.

Some indication of the difference in the level of use of public transport in different areas can be obtained from figures given in the National Transport Survey. These are shown in Table 4.

Table 4. Use of public transport analysed by area: journey stages and mileage[1]

Mode	London transport area		Other conurbations		Other urban areas		Non-urban areas	
	Journey stages %	Mileage %	Journey stages %	Mileage %	Journey stages %	Mileage %	Journey stages %	Mileage %
British Rail	5.6	11.4	1.9	5.3	1.5	7.7	1.5	4.6
London Underground	8.8	9.1	—	—	—	—	—	—
Local bus	26.8	13.4	46.4	31.0	34.3	23.8	18.0	15.2
Other public transport	1.2	2.5	1.1	2.7	6.9	1.6	0.8	0.6
Total public transport	42.4	36.4	49.4	39.0	36.7	33.1[2]	20.5	20.4[4]
Private car	31.7	45.8	28.4	44.3	30.0	46.3	43.6	56.9
Other private transport	26.1	17.7	21.1	16.7	33.0	20.4	35.9	22.5
Total private transport	57.8	63.5	50.5	61.0	63.0	66.7[3]	79.5	79.4
TOTAL	100.2	99.9	99.9	100.0	99.7	99.8	100.0	99.8

[1]National Travel Survey, 1964. Ministry of Transport Preliminary Report, Part II, Tables 20A and 21A; [2]shown as 33.0 in N.T.S. Table; [3]shown as 63.3 in N.T.S. Table; [4]shown as 20.6 in N.T.S. Table.

There are several interesting features shown by these figures. As would be expected rail is relatively more important when measured by mileage rather than journey stages but public transport as a whole is less important because

* *Passenger Transport in Great Britain*, 1965, Table 41.
† *Ibid.*, Table 42.

the average bus journey is shorter than the average car journey. The total share of public transport in London is less than that in other conurbations, and this would suggest that the existence of the London underground reduces the number of people who would otherwise travel by bus but does not lead to any reduction in the use of private cars. It must of course be remembered that these figures relate to total passenger transport and that the position for the journey to work, which is discussed below, may be different. The statistics in Table 4 also support the not unexpected conclusion that public transport is less important in the smaller towns and in rural areas than it is in London and the other conurbations. Some other evidence of regional variation in the use of public transport is contained in figures shown diagrammatically in the 1965 Transport Holding Company Report. These figures, which relate only to traffic to and from the city centre, and are estimates which must be interpreted with considerable caution are shown in Table 5, together with figures contained in the Ministry of Transport Report *Better Use of Town Roads*.

Table 5. Estimated comparisons of rail, car and bus shares of passenger transport, to and from city centres[1]

Town	Rail	Bus and coach	Car and motor cycle	Other (including walking)	Total
A. % of passenger miles, 1965					
Bristol	2.5	48.6	48.9	—	100.0
Glasgow	15.9	69.8	14.3	—	100.0
Liverpool	21.8	61.4	16.8	—	100.0
Newcastle upon Tyne	6.3	73.3	18.4	—	100.0
B. % of journeys at peak periods					
Birmingham	24.0	65.0	11.0	—	100.0
Cardiff	23.0	30.0	32.0	15.0	100.0
Leeds	14.0	65.0	19.0	2.0	100.0
Reading	—	46.0	45.0	9.0	100.0

[1]Figures in A. estimated from Transport Holding Company Report, 1965, Diagram 7, p. 30. Figures in B. taken from Table 3-4, *Better Use of Town Roads*, p. 11.

Even if there is some inaccuracy in these estimates and allowing for the impreciseness of the concept 'city centre' the differences are so great as to suggest considerable real differences between towns in modal split. It would be extremely interesting to analyse all the reasons why, for example, only 11% of peak hour travellers used private cars in Birmingham while 45%

did so in Reading. According to the recent report *Cars for Cities*, 'The larger the town, the smaller is the proportion of commuters using private transport,'* and this point is also made in the *Better Use of Town Roads* report.† This conclusion is not, however, supported by any very adequate statistical analysis, and there are certainly other important variables such as the level of car ownership. The *Cars for Cities* report gives some absolute figures of commuter traffic in 1962 which suggest that the total number of commuters may have a variable relationship with population, though the report does not comment on this point. The approximate figures are shown in Table 6.

Table 6. Number of commuters and population, provincial towns, 1962[1]

Town	No. of commuters (approx.) per day, 1962	Population 1961	Commuters per head of population
Glasgow	155,000	1,054,913	0.15
Manchester	138,000	661,041	0.21
Newcastle upon Tyne	70,000	269,389	0.26
Leicester	50,000	273,298	0.18
Cardiff	40,000	256,270	0.16
Luton	25,000	131,505	0.19
Doncaster	21,000	86,402	0.24
Coventry	18,000	305,060	0.06

[1]*Cars for Cities*, Fig. 3:1, p. 22.

The position of towns like Coventry suggests the need for an analysis distinguishing between the effects of total population and total commuter traffic on the choice between public and private transport. The figures for

Table 7. Journeys into central London on working days in 1962[1]

Mode	All day	Morning peak
	%	%
Car and motor cycle	20.5	12.5
Bus and coach	27.5	23.0
Rail	49.8	64.0
Taxi	2.0	0.3
Goods vehicle	0.2	0.2
TOTAL	100.0	100.0

[1]*Better Use of Town Roads*, p. 10.

personal journeys into central London for the whole day and for the morning peak periods are shown in Table 7.

* *Cars for Cities*, Ministry of Transport, 1967, p. 22.
† *Better Use of Town Roads*, p. 11.

The National Travel Survey showed that 32% of all mileage travelled by people included in the sample was undertaken by public transport* and this agrees fairly closely with the estimate of 33.3% for 1964 contained in *Passenger Transport in Great Britain.*†

In order to analyse such problems as the relation of total passenger flow to the flow at peak periods and the possibility of bringing about changes in modal split it is important to know something about the main purpose for which people travel. Table 8 shows estimates for the purpose of travel based on the National Travel Survey sample.

Table 8. The purpose of passenger travel, 1964[1]

Purpose	Journey stages	Mileage
	%	%
To and from work	38.0	30.5
In course of work	4.0	7.9
To and from school or college	8.8	5.1
Shopping and personal business	17.5	13.1
Entertainment, sport, eating and drinking	8.8	8.3
Personal social travel	14.6	19.5
Other personal travel (holidays, pleasure, etc.)	8.3	15.5
	100.0	99.9

[1]National Travel Survey, *op. cit.*, Tables 10A and 10B.

The journey to work is therefore of outstanding importance, as the main reason why people travel, and because a very large part of this travelling will be in urban areas, and is also likely to be the main constituent of demand peaks. It is generally even more important for public than for private transport. Table 9 shows the estimated percentages of total journey stage and mileage for different transport modes which were to or from work in 1964.

It is perhaps a little surprising that British Rail passenger services are more heavily dependent on commuter traffic than the bus services and that even when measured by mileage over 40% of rail passenger traffic is for journeys

* National Travel Survey, *op. cit.*, Part II, p. (v)

† Table 2, p. 2. These figures include inland air transport (0.5% of total passenger mileage).

Table 9. The importance of journeys to and from work for different transport modes, 1964[1]

Mode	Percentage of total journey stages	Percentage of total mileage
British Rail	56.7	41.6
L. T. Underground	63.7	64.8
London buses	44.9	43.6
Other buses	38.5	37.6
Car (as driver)	37.4	28.5
Car (as passenger)	21.0	13.0

[1]National Travel Survey, *op. cit.*, Tables 10A and 11A.

between home and work. The work journey is responsible for a larger proportion of traffic on London Transport buses than on 'other' buses but this figure would be influenced by the inclusion of rural bus services under the latter heading. The much higher percentage of car driver traffic than car passenger traffic represented by the journey to work is reflected in the lower

Table 10. The journey to work analysed by mode of transport, Great Britain, 1964[1]

Transport mode	Percentage of total journey stages	Percentage of total mileage
British Rail	3.5	10.1
L.T. Underground	3.4	4.3
London Transport bus	6.6	3.7
Other bus	27.0	22.6
Other (including taxis)	0.6	0.8
Total public transport	41.4	41.5
Private bus	1.5	3.5
Car (as driver)	18.9	24.5
Car (as passenger)	7.3	9.4
Goods vehicle (as passenger)	1.7	3.4
Goods vehicle (as driver)	3.1	4.5
Motor cycle, scooter or moped	4.5	5.0
Bicycle and other private transport	13.7	5.8
Walking (over one mile)	7.9	2.4
Total private transport	58.6	58.5
TOTAL	100.0	100.0

[1]National Travel Survey, *op. cit.*, Tables 1A and 2A.

rate of car occupancy at peak periods when the work journey is most important. In Table 10 the journey to and from work is analysed according to the modal split.

Rather more than half the journeys were made by private transport by either method of measurement. As was the case with the total travel figures, rail and private car became more important when measured by mileage rather than journey stages.

The central problem of urban passenger transport is, then, that the demand for travel is greater than can be met without seriously reducing the quality of the service supplied. In particular road space is over-used in every large town (and many smaller ones) in Britain. There are many possible short-term and long-term answers to the problem. Towns can be redesigned to make it easier for people to live near central work areas; work opportunities can be moved away from town centres; working, shopping and school hours can be altered to reduce the peakedness of demand; the supply of road space can be increased by road improvements and new building; traffic engineering techniques can be adopted to enable a given traffic flow to move faster without increasing road space; small 'city cars' making an economical use of road space can be developed; and people can be persuaded to use public rather than private transport. It is with achieving this last objective that this study is mainly concerned.

There are two main methods of bringing about a greater use of public transport, persuasion and constraint. Persuasion involves making public transport more attractive. The main method of doing this considered here is by altering the external factors affecting bus operation; by possible changes in the licensing regulations and the present system of imposing rigid boundaries on the routes operated by individual undertakings, and by changing the financial structure of the industry which makes it necessary for some undertakings to 'cross-subsidize' their rural services from earnings on urban routes. The possibility of a state or local authority subsidy for undertakings is also considered. But since there is very strong evidence to suggest that persuasion alone is inadequate, a considerable part of the study is devoted to examining the possibility of using some forms of constraint to limit the free use of private cars, in particular on the very important journey to work.

2

Passenger transport in Leicester

The case study of passenger traffic on which this book is based related to 'Greater Leicester' and comprised the City of Leicester itself and the continuously built up area around the city. The Leicester Traffic Plan defined Greater Leicester as '. . . not only the City of Leicester and its built-up fringe, but also those areas beyond where development is now taking place, or where it is likely to take place in the future on a reasonably substantial scale.'* This is a rather imprecise definition but it was delineated by a cordon line 'selected jointly by the City and County Planning Officers.'† This line and also that of the built-up area, are shown approximately in Figure 1. For population comparison purposes it is convenient to define 'Greater Leicester' as Leicester City, Oadby and Wigston Urban Districts, and Barrow-upon-Soar, Billesdon and Blaby Rural Districts. (This includes some rural areas outside the zone of continuous urban development and excludes Market Bosworth R.D.C., a small part of which is inside the Leicester Traffic Plan cordon.) Population changes in these areas are shown in Table 11,

Table 11. Population changes, Greater Leicester, 1951–65.

Year	Inner Leicester	Outer Leicester	Greater Leicester
1951	285,181	116,093	401,274
1961	273,470	165,471	438,941
1964[1]	267,050	184,560	451,610
1965[1]	267,015	190,869	457,884

[1]Registrar General's estimate, 30 June 1964 and 30 June 1965.

where 'Inner Leicester' means the City of Leicester, and 'Outer Leicester' the other two Urban and three Rural Districts.

Thus the population of the City of Leicester declined by 18,166, or 6.37%,

* W. K. Smigielski, *Leicester Traffic Plan*, 1964, p. 9.
† *Ibid.*, p. 8.

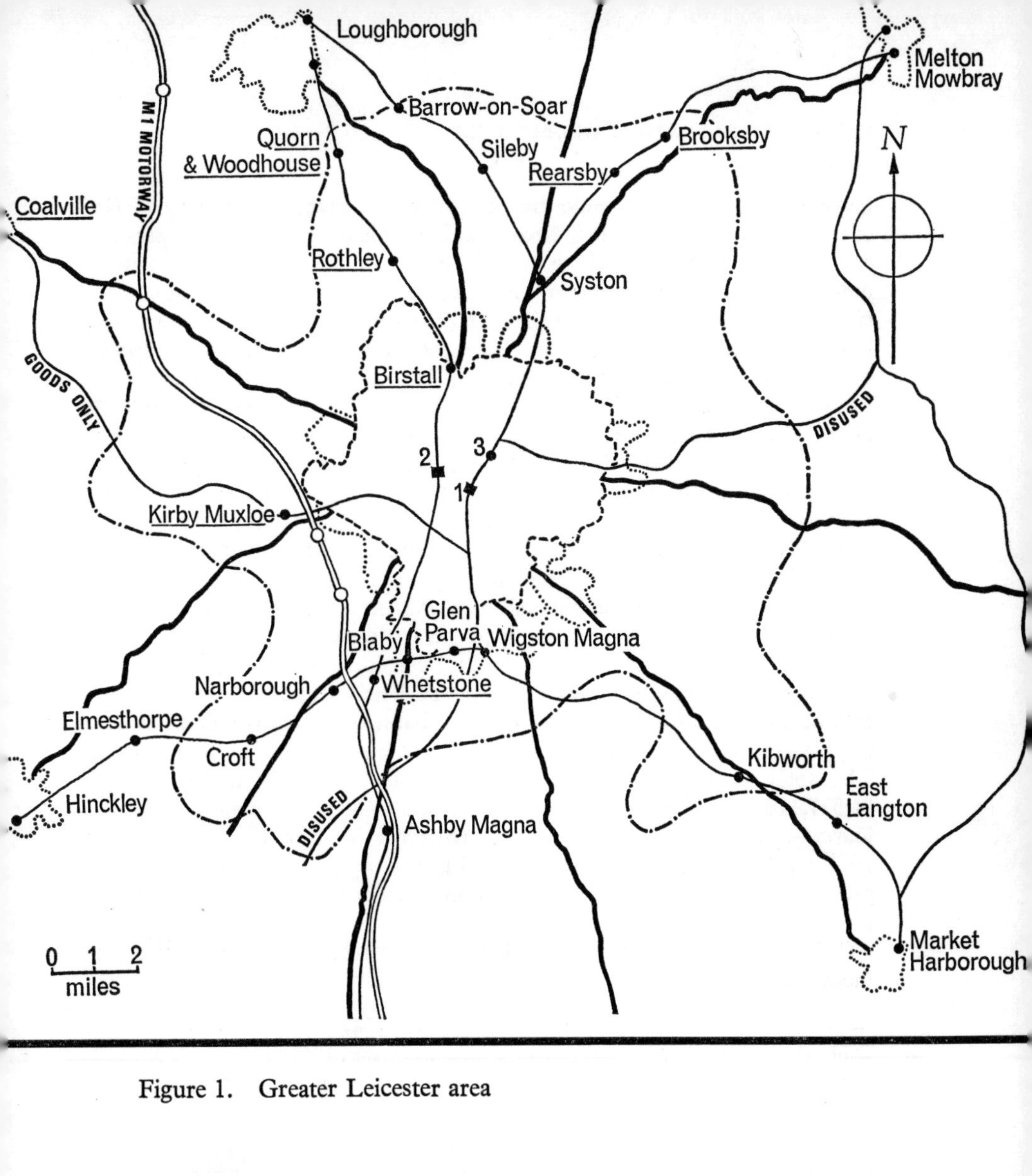

Figure 1. Greater Leicester area

main roads

Leicester cordon area

other built-up areas

railways

Leicester boundary

Rothley

station closed

between 1951 and 1965, while that of 'Outer Leicester' increased by 74,776, or 64.41% in the same period. Greater Leicester had a gain of 56,610 persons, or 14.11%. These figures show that Leicester has experienced the growth of outer suburban development with a (smaller) decline in the population of the central areas which is typical of the larger urban centres in Britain during the last sixteen years. The overall decline in the City population was not spread evenly over the wards. Much the largest decline, between 1951 and 1961, was in inner wards like St Margarets (–7644) and The Castle (–5476), while six of the sixteen wards increased their population in this period. The increase in the population of the Rural Districts round Leicester was almost entirely concentrated in the suburbs on the fringe of the City. Thus in Blaby Rural District the total population increase between 1951 and 1961 was 17,210. But the total increase in five Civil Parishes bordering the City (Blaby, Braunstone, Glenfield, Glen Parva and Kirby Muxloe) was 16,016, leaving a net gain of only 1,194 for the remaining eighteen Parishes. The obvious transport implications are that the demand for longer journeys into and out of the city centre area might be expected to increase considerably while that from the inner suburbs remains stationary or declines. The only part of the passenger transport demand for which figures are available on a comparable basis over the period 1951–64 is that which was carried by the City bus undertaking. The total passengers carried declined from 99,248,039 in 1951–52 to 86,577,110 in 1961–62 and to 82,841,454 in 1964–65. The annual passenger journeys per head of population were therefore 348.0 in 1951–52, 316.8 in 1961–62 and 310.2 in 1964/65. The fall in this figure presumably reflects a greater use of private cars since there is no evidence that the demand per head for travel has fallen.

Table 12 shows estimates of the daily passenger flow by different transport modes in Greater Leicester.

Table 12. Estimated daily traffic flows, Greater Leicester, 1965/66

Mode	Low estimate No. of passenger trips	%	High estimate No. of passenger trips	%
Bus	357,700	46.0	380,500	41.4
Train	5,600	0.7	7,400	0.8
Private car	415,000	53.3	530,700	57.8
TOTAL	778,300	100.0	918,600	100.0

The 'low' estimate for bus passengers is based on Tuesday and Friday flows, the 'high' estimate on Saturday figures. The train figures were based on a weekly survey and on annual returns. The car figures must be considered much more approximate than those for bus and train passengers as they were estimated from sample figures in the Leicester Traffic Plan, projected forward to 1966 for the 'high' estimate. Bus circular trips are included. According to the Leicester Traffic Plan figures for 1963 24.9% of all trips inside the 'cordon area' were made by bus, 0.2% by train and 29.0% by private car and motor cycle. If the 34.7% of walking trips and 9.3% pedal cycle trips are eliminated these figures become bus 44.6%, train 0.4%, car and motor cycle 52.9%, and 'other' (drivers and passengers in commercial vehicles and taxi passengers) 2.0%. For inward trips between 8 and 9 A.M. the corresponding figures were: bus 64.0%, car and motor cycle 34.6%, and train 1.4%.

These figures of traffic inside the Leicester Traffic Plan 'cordon' would exclude commuter traffic from the surrounding country and may thus be expected to underestimate the importance of rail traffic and probably also of private car traffic.

The division of bus passengers between the two major undertakings is shown in Table 13.

Table 13.
Division of bus passengers between Midland Red and Leicester City Transport

Date	Passengers carried during working day	
	Midland Red	City
Saturday, 15 May 1965		268,087
Friday, 24 September 1965		259,697
Saturday, 2 April 1966	112,410	
Tuesday, 9 April 1966	97,983	
Average	105,196.5	263,892

If these passenger counts are accepted as representative* then the City undertaking was carrying approximately 71.5% and the Midland Red undertaking 28.5% of the passenger flow. This is not, however, a satisfactory measure of the work done by the two undertakings since the average mileage of the Midland Red would be expected to be higher than that of the City undertaking. The average revenue per passenger for the City was 4.06*d.* (on

* Figures are available for the three main Midland Red garages for a Tuesday and these showed that the flow was higher than on a Friday (87,196 for Tuesday, 29 March 1966, 81,036 for Friday, 8 April 1966).

24 September 65) while that for the Midland Red ranged from 9.0*d.* to 12.4*d.* per passenger for different garages. The Midland Red average revenue for the three main Leicester garages for three days (29 March 66, 2 April 66 and 8 April 66) was 10.4*d.* per passenger. This reflects both longer journeys and the higher charges per mile on Midland Red services necessitated by the need to cross-subsidize rural routes. If passenger trips are weighted by revenue per passenger then the Midland Red share of the passenger transport 'work done' becomes 50.3% and that of the City undertaking 49.7%.

In so far as a comparison is possible between the various estimates of modal split for Leicester and those for other towns shown in Table 5 it would seem that the situation in Leicester is reasonably typical, except for the very small proportion of passenger traffic using the railways. The organization of bus services in Leicester is relatively simple in that Leicester is not part of a conurbation and it does not have the multiplicity of services operated by different undertakings found in Lancashire, or, to a lesser extent, in the Black Country. There are some small undertakings operating private bus services mainly serving works and the stage services of the Trent and Barton undertaking running in from Nottingham but otherwise the great bulk of public bus transport is in the hands of the Corporation and Midland Red undertakings. 'Midland Red,' or the Birmingham and Midland Motor Omnibus Company, is the largest undertaking in Britain, apart from London Transport, with an area extending from the Welsh border to the East Midlands.

Midland Red is part of the British Electric Traction Group, and 50% of its ordinary share capital is owned by the state through the Transport Holding Company. In the country as a whole the Transport Holding Company is responsible wholly or partially for approximately 80% of all stage services apart from those of London Transport and the municipal undertakings.* The wholly owned Tilling Group operates in six main areas: Eastern, East Midland, Northern, North Western, Western and South Wales and Southern. The Holding Company also owns the Scottish Bus Group operating buses over most of Scotland. The individual companies in the East Midland group are the Lincolnshire Road Car Co., the Mansfield District Tractor Co., the Midland General Omnibus Co., the Nottinghamshire and Derbyshire Traction Co., and the United Counties Omnibus Co. Some degree of public ownership is therefore very widespread in the industry, but in practice there is no direct government interference with the operators of partially-owned subsidiaries like Midland Red. Two of the eight directors of

* Transport Holding Company Report, 1966, p. 27.

Midland Red are connected with the Transport Holding Company: Sir Reginald Wilson is deputy chairman of the T.H.C. and Mr H. E. Osborn is comptroller of T.H.C. and also a director of British Road Services. Three Midland Red directors are directors of the British Electric Traction Group and three (including the chairman) are also directors of Rediffusion Ltd., which is a subsidiary of British Electric Traction. The Leicester District of Midland Red is in charge of a traffic superintendent with offices and staff in Leicester and there are also officers in the company's Birmingham headquarters with special responsibility for Leicester District.

The average fleet size of Transport Holding Company undertakings was 590 in 1966, and that of 95 municipal undertakings in Britain was 190 vehicles.* Leicester Corporation undertaking had a fleet of 210 vehicles in 1966 with a total seating capacity of 14,188.

The road transport situation in Leicester was thus fairly typical for Britain, with a municipal undertaking serving most of the city and a company undertaking serving the outer suburbs and having services running out into the country. As is shown more fully later the amount of joint operation of services is probably rather less in Leicester than in many other large towns. The railways are also less important for carrying commuter traffic into Leicester than they are in some comparable urban areas.

* T.H.C. Report, 1966, p. 28.

3

Costs and prices

In this chapter the cost structure of bus undertakings is examined and the problem of 'unremunerative' services and of cross subsidization is considered. The costs and prices of public and private passenger transport are also compared.

According to statements made to the Jack Committee on Rural Bus Services, 32% of the total mileage and 64% of the services operated by the Midland Red Company were 'unremunerative' in 1958, and the position has since deteriorated. But 'unremunerative' is defined in the Report as failure to meet 'average overall costs' and subsequent evidence from the Public Transport Association admitted that some unremunerative services may '. . . contribute something beyond their bare running costs towards the overhead expenses of the undertaking.'* This distinction between overall costs and 'bare running costs' is approximately equivalent to the economist's concepts of average and marginal cost. In the greatly simplified model of the firm used in much of economic analysis marginal cost is the cost of producing an extra unit of output and it can be shown that the firm will increase its profits by increasing sales so long as the extra revenue from an extra unit sold is greater than the marginal costs involved. The sale of such a unit of output cannot therefore be called unremunerative. The difficulty about applying this argument to the real world of transport is that there is no clearly identifiable quantity which can be recognized as marginal cost; or it could be argued, there are a whole series of different marginal costs according to the definition given to that other elusive concept, a unit of output. But the basic principle is certainly relevant. If the revenue which can be obtained from providing a service is greater than the cost which could be escaped by not providing it, then it would pay a profit-maximizing undertaking to provide it. If instead of a profit-maximizing firm we have a 'public service' seeking only to cover its costs then so long as escapable costs are covered, there is no misallocation of resources. Thus if the alternative to running a particular bus trip is for the

* Report of the Committee on Rural Bus Services, Ministry of Transport, 1961, pp. 25–26.

bus and its crew to be idle in the garage, then it is profitable to run it for a revenue of about 6*d.* per mile (assuming that this covers fuel costs and any additional servicing and maintenance costs arising from the trip) even if the average total costs of the undertaking were 45*d.* per vehicle mile. Although other trips on the same route were yielding a revenue of 70*d.* per vehicle mile there would not, in these circumstances, be any cross-subsidization involved. The practical problem is, of course, to be able to decide which costs are dependent on the running or not-running of a particular service.

In the very short run period, when no alterations to the bus service can be made at all, 'marginal cost' (this term will now be used to denote the costs which would be avoided if a service was not operated, even where that service is the operation of a complete bus route) is virtually nil. If a bus stops to pick up eight passengers then the cost of allowing a ninth on to the bus is the fraction of extra time involved plus a negligible addition to fuel costs, and it would be worth while to carry this passenger at almost any fare, if a separate bargain could be made with him. (This also assumes that there will always be spare seats on the bus on this particular trip, and that the ninth passenger will alight at the same stop as at least one other passenger.) Suppose next that the decision about whether or not a particular bus trip should run in an off-peak period could be made at a few minutes' notice. If the trip (from the cost point of view a trip must normally be defined as a completed outward and return journey, though the situation could be envisaged where a driver was ordered to switch to a different incoming route) was cancelled, the fuel costs, costs of tyre wear, and the non-labour part of the costs of repairs, maintenance, and cleaning attributable to that trip could be saved. If a particular trip was taken out of the timetable permanently then probably the labour content of repairs, maintenance and cleaning costs could be saved as well. Whether or not the much more important item of drivers' and conductors' wages could be saved in these circumstances depends on a number of factors. The longer the missed trip the more likely it would be that the driver and conductor could be used elsewhere. The driver's and conductor's wages would probably be saved if the removed trip was at a peak period; if it was at an off-peak time they would be more likely to spend the time idle. The next stage of marginal costs would come if a whole route, or a number of trips, were taken from the timetable. Drivers' and conductors' wages would now almost certainly be saved, and also the size of the bus fleet could usually be reduced. This would bring in the items of renewals and depreciation of capital equipment and any loan charges attributable to the no-longer-required vehicles. (If the vehicles could not be sold there would eventually be a saving when fewer new buses than otherwise required would be bought.) Again the place in the timetable of the removed services would be important; on any service affected by peaks in demand the removal of off-peak services will not lead to any reduction in the fleet size. This analysis could be continued further by taking longer time periods, when some overhead costs might be escaped if services were reduced. Office staff might be cut, for example, or one garage closed down. But the difficulties of generalizing about marginal cost have already been illustrated. There are strictly, an almost infinite series of marginal costs varying with the very many different types of unit of output which may or may not be produced.*

The preceding arguments do not mean, however, that no generalization at all can be made about the relationship between specific outputs of a bus undertaking, and their costs. For the purposes of this study five initial 'cost levels' can be distinguished. These cumulative levels of cost are set out below.

Cost Level A

Fuel cost (including tax)+repairs and maintenance of vehicles+tyres+cleaning and lubricating vehicles.

Cost Level B

A+drivers' and conductors' wages+uniforms.

Cost Level C

A+B+provision for renewal and depreciation of vehicles+local authority provision for debt redemption.

Cost Level D

A+B+C+all other costs except interest payments.

Cost Level E

A+B+C+D+interest payments+capital expenditure from revenue other than that on vehicles.

Cost level A represents the costs which might be escaped if a bus did not undertake a particular trip, and the bus and crew remained idle in the garage. This cost level could be subdivided in a more refined analysis according to whether or not labour costs are included. Thus if a bus does not need to be

* This does not mean merely that because of indivisibilities marginal cost varies for different sized 'lumps' of output, but that, given the existing size of the undertaking, the marginal cost of an extra unit of one bus mile would differ according to the time of day or the route concerned. This virtually amounts to admitting that there is no such thing as a marginal cost curve for a bus undertaking.

cleaned, the costs of any power and materials will be saved, but whether or not the labour costs of the cleaning staff will be saved depends upon circumstances. Costs of level B would be avoided if besides all the savings of level A, the bus drivers' and conductors' wages could be saved. This would be made possible if they could be used on another route, and overtime saved, or if they were running the removed trip on overtime, or (as might happen where the complete services on a route were withdrawn) if the total bus-crew of the undertaking could be reduced. Costs of level C could be escaped if, in addition to the above savings, the size of the bus fleet could be reduced. Cost level D is equivalent to what is generally called 'Total Working Expenses' in municipal accounts, plus capital expenditure paid out of revenue, which is taken to be the equivalent of depreciation where this item does not occur. Finally cost level E represents total costs (though without any allowance for the accumulation of a surplus for new investment).

Fitting actual figures to these cost levels is difficult for two main reasons. One is that accounting practices differ considerably, particularly in the allocation of labour costs. Some municipal undertakings include all labour costs other than those directly related to traffic operation under some such heading as 'General Expenses' while others allocate them to specific activities like fuel distribution and repairs and maintenance. Similarly the treatment of national insurance and superannuation payments varies. Thus the total cost of servicing vehicles and routes for Leicester City undertaking in 1965–66 was £47,248 or 1.624*d.* per vehicle mile. But of this total £33,799 or 1.16*d.* per vehicle mile was represented by the four labour costs, wages, national insurance, superannuation and sick pay. The other problem is that operating conditions of different undertakings will differ very considerably in ways which will affect costs. The main cost-affecting factors will be the rate of wages which must be paid, the average speed obtainable from buses, the make-up of the bus fleet (single decker buses will have lower operating costs, but also, of course, lower revenue potential), the proportion of peak to non-peak working, and the nature of the terrain over which services are run. It is also possible that undertakings which have suffered a severe recent fall in passenger mileage may not have yet been able to make all the possible reductions in overhead costs. The accounts of individual company undertakings are not usually set out in sufficient detail for all of the cost levels listed to be applied.

The first set of figures analysed are shown in Tables 14–16 and are based on figures returned by undertakings to the Ministry of Transport.

Table 14. Cost levels, London Transport

Cost Level	1962/63	1963/64 *d.* per vehicle mile	1964/65
a	4.71	4.66	4.71
A	6.69	6.73	6.83
b	20.80	21.17	24.68
B	27.48	27.90	31.51
C	29.50	29.84	33.15
D	43.61	44.81	49.81

Table 15. Cost levels, local authorities undertakings

Cost Level	1962/63	1963/64 *d.* per vehicle mile	1964/65
a	4.50	4.68	4.77
A	6.37	6.65	6.86
b	16.55	18.44	20.11
B	22.91	25.09	26.69
C	24.69	27.30	29.21
D	36.15	39.61	42.44

Table 16. Cost levels, company undertakings

Cost Level	1962/63	1963/64 *d.* per vehicle mile	1964/65
a	3.70	3.73	3.68
A	5.42	5.53	5.57
b	13.09	13.71	14.76
B	18.51	19.24	20.33
C	20.50	21.32	22.54
D	28.43	29.71	31.51

The figures in these Tables were calculated from the data on Traffic and Operation (Table 28) and Receipts and Expenditure of operators of more than 24 buses and coaches (Table 29) in *Passenger Transport in Great Britain*, 1962, 1963, and 1964. They include Express services, Excursions and tours and Contract work as well as Stage services. In each case expenditure figures relating to financial years ending up to 31 March of the later year shown were divided by vehicle mileage figures for that year. Thus 1964/65 expenditure figures were divided by 1965 vehicle mileages. The figures were recalculated using vehicle mileages from the earlier calendar year, but in no case did this change them very much. Figures for cost level E were not available. 'a' refers to fuel costs and 'b' to drivers' and conductors' wages.

The absolute levels of the figures for company undertakings cannot be compared with those for local authorities and London Transport as they include a much greater proportion of Express services, Excursions and tours and Contract work. These operations will have a quite different, and generally much lower cost structure (in terms of cost per vehicle miles) than Stage services. It is not clear how far these national statistics prepared by the Ministry of Transport allow for vagaries in different accounting systems. It would appear that labour costs have not generally been allocated to such items as Repairs and Maintenance.

The cost figures for Leicester City Transport are shown in Table 17.

Table 17. Cost structure of Leicester City Transport

	Cost (*d.* per vehicle mile)		
Cost Level	1963/64	1964/65	1965/66
a	5.177	5.097	5.047
A	10.925	10.768	10.900
b	21.501	22.344	24.517
B	32.711	33.420	35.417
C[1]	35.221	36.251	39.935
D	41.808	43.389	47.660
E	41.808	43.731	49.413

[1]Non-vehicular capital expenditure from revenue was included at C.

If for 1965/66 the costs of wages and salaries, national insurance, superannuation and sick pay were removed from the items power, servicing vehicles and routes and repairs and maintenance of vehicles, the result would be to reduce cost level A to approximately 6.7*d.* per vehicle mile, B to 31.217*d.* and C to 35.735*d.* Cost levels D and E would remain the same since the labour costs would be added in at level D. Power costs in 1965/66 without the labour element would be reduced to 4.981*d.* per vehicle mile. The capital expenditure brought in partly at C and partly at E was more than twice the average figure in 1965/66 so that the increase does not necessarily reflect an upward trend.

Tables 18–20 show the variation in fuel expenses, drivers' and conductors' wages, and total working expenses for municipal undertakings in 1963/64.

Table 18. Fuel cost of municipal undertakings, 1963/64

Cost (*d.* per vehicle mile)	No. of undertakings
Less than 4.0	1
4.0 – 4.49	16
4.5 – 4.99	44
5.0 – 5.49	30
5.5 – 5.99	2
6.0 and over	1
TOTAL	94

The figure for Leicester City Transport was 5.18*d.* per vehicle mile.

Table 19. Drivers' and conductors, wages costs of municipal undertakings. 1963/64

Cost (*d.* per vehicle mile)	No. of undertakings
Less than 14.0	2
14 – 15.99	12
16 – 17.99	31
18 – 19.99	31
20 – 21.99	16
22.0 and over	2
TOTAL	94

The figure for Leicester City Transport was 19.21*d.* per vehicle mile.

Table 20. Total working expenses of municipal undertakings, 1963/64

Cost (*d.* per vehicle mile)	No. of undertakings
Less than 30.0	2
30 – 34.99	20
35 – 39.99	41
40 – 44.99	25
45 – 49.99	6
50 – 54.99	0
55 – 59.99	0
60.0 and over	1
TOTAL	95

The figure for Leicester City Transport was 39.29*d.* per vehicle mile.

Figures for the Midland Red organization are shown in Table 21.

Table 21. Cost structure of the Midland Red organization

Cost Level	1964	1965
a	4.00	3.94
A	—	—
b	16.46	17.45
B	—	—
C	—	—
D	35.24	37.73
E	—	—

It is not easy to fit individual company figures into the A–E categories, partly because of lack of data and partly through differences in company accounting practice. At the level of total costs the position of local authorities and companies is not exactly comparable. Interest payment on loan capital is shown as a cost, but not dividend payments on Ordinary Shares. Since local authorities only have loan capital this tends to overstate local authority total costs relative to those of companies. On the other hand the repayment of debt by local authorities means that their outstanding debt is generally less than that of the total capitalization of companies (including Ordinary Shares issued). Leicester City undertaking has repaid all its outstanding debt, and in 1964/65 and 1965/66 bank charges were less than the interest received by the undertaking. The position is further complicated in that part of the provision for debt redemption by local authorities is really the equivalent of allowances for renewal and depreciation made by companies.

The relationship of the Midland Red figures to the operating costs of this undertaking in the Leicester area is uncertain for two reasons. First, as with almost all company undertakings, they include a proportion of Express services and Contract work which, as indicated above, normally have considerably lower 'per vehicle mile' costs than Stage services. Secondly, the undertaking covers a very wide area, ranging from Herefordshire, where the generally uncongested roads should give lower costs than in Leicester, to Birmingham and the Black Country where congestion may often be worse and costs possibly higher than in Leicester. A considerable number of Midland Red routes operating from Leicester ran out into the country and thus had two sections with differing cost and revenue conditions.

The revenue-cost relationship of bus undertakings can be analysed at various levels which include the position of the whole undertaking, the position of separate routes, and that of individual bus trips. Data is available for all undertakings on their overall annual position; that for routes and trips has had to be constructed from basic data such as drivers' time sheets, and it has only been possible to deal with the situation on individual days.

Leicester City undertaking achieved net surpluses of £29,049, £29,063 and £2,496 in 1963/64, 1964/65 and 1965/66 respectively. The total working expenses in the same three financial years were £1,140,184, £1,184,485 and £1,255,306. The Midland Red made a net profit before taxation of £1,043,903 in 1964 and £726,828 in 1965 (year ended 31 December). The corresponding figures for total expenditure before tax were £11,152,194 and £11,319,641, so that profits were equal to 9.36% and 6.42% of total expenditure in 1964 and 1965 respectively. Table 22 shows the net difference between receipts and expenditure for all undertakings included in the Ministry of Transport returns.

Table 22. Difference between receipts and expenditure; operators of more than 24 buses and coaches (£ thousands)

	1962/63	1963/64	1964/65
London Transport	5045	3863	2163
Local Authorities	2863	2868	2515
Companies	13,474	13,919	14,575

These figures show that the financial position of the company undertakings was consistently more healthy than that of municipal undertakings or London Transport. In 1964/65 company undertakings had a net surplus of £0.096 for each £1 of expenditure, while the corresponding figure for local authority undertakings was £0.026.

Table 23 shows the profit or loss position of a number of local authority undertakings.

Table 23. Net surplus/loss, municipal transport undertakings, 1963–66

Year	Loss or Surplus (£)						Total
	−10,000 or more	−1000 −9999	0 −999	0 +999	+1000 +9999	+10,000 or more	
1963/64	1	2	1	—	5	3	12
1964/65	15	9	—	4	16	19	63
1965/66	12	12	1	3	11	24	63
TOTAL	28	23	2	7	32	46	138

This series is not, of course, long enough for any trend to be established. The percentage of undertakings making a net loss was almost the same in 1964/65 (38%) and in 1965/66 (39.7%). Some undertakings swung dramatically from a deficit to a surplus (*e.g.*, Aberdeen, 1964/65 deficit=£22,451; 1965/66 surplus=£95,909) or vice versa (*e.g.*, Kingston upon Hull, 1964/65 surplus=£4,562; 1965/66 deficit=£98,340; Sunderland, 1964/65 surplus=£106,068; 1965/66 deficit=£79,766). Many undertakings had considerable losses in 1964/65 and in 1965/66 (*e.g.*, Coventry, £50,573; £157,126; Liverpool, £42,371; £110,298; Merthyr Tydfil, £46,189; £62,397; St Helens, £67,556; £72,067) while others had large surpluses in both these years (*e.g.*, Manchester, £104,799; £211,573; Newcastle upon Tyne, £156,643; £191,499; Portsmouth, £93,099; £51,086; Sheffield, £304,972; £132,110). There appeared to be no clear relationship between the size of undertakings and their degree of financial success.

As has already been pointed out, company undertaking results cannot be compared directly with those of local authorities because of the different method of financing operations. Nevertheless a small number of company accounts were analysed for comparison with each other. Out of fifteen companies analysed in 1963/64 only one did not have a net surplus after taxation, and the average net surplus was £173,791.7. Nineteen company undertaking accounts for 1964/65 were analysed and these showed no net deficits and an average surplus after tax of £173,426.3.

The route revenue of Leicester City Transport routes is shown in Table 24.

Table 24. Route revenue, Leicester City Transport, 1965

Revenue *d.* per mile	No. of routes Fri., 24 September	Sat., 1 May	Sun. 28 March
Less than 10	0	1	0
10.0 – 32.9	1	3	19
33.0 – 35.9	0	2	4
36.0 – 43.9	17	11	12
44.0 and over	35	34	13
TOTAL	53	51	48

These figures are arranged according to an estimate of cost levels A, B, C and E based on 1964/65 costs per vehicle mile for Leicester City Transport. A rearrangement of the same revenue figures according to cost levels based on 1965/66 Leicester City costs, and bringing in cost level D, is shown in Table 25.

Table 25. Route revenue, Leicester City Transport, second analysis, 1965

Revenue *d.* per mile	No. of routes Fri., 24 September	Sat., 1 May	Sun., 28 March
Less than 11	0	1	0
11 – 35.9	1	5	23
36 – 39.9	7	6	8
40 – 47.9	18	7	7
48 – 49.9	0	3	1
50 and over	27	29	9
TOTAL	53	51	48

Route figures for 91 Midland Red services operating from Leicester are analysed according to two different cost levels in Table 26.

Table 26. Route revenue, Midland Red services running into Leicester, 29 March 1966

Revenue	No. of routes	Revenue	No. of routes
Less than 6.0	1	Less than 11.0	1
6.0 – 23.9	14	11.0 – 35.9	42
24.0 – 26.9	7	36.0 – 39.9	15
27.0 – 34.9	19	40.0 – 47.9	18
35.0 – 37.9	6	48.0 – 49.9	4
38.0 and over	44	50.0 and over	11
TOTAL	91	TOTAL	91

The first set of figures fitted to the cost levels in Table 26 are based on the overall costs of the Midland Red undertaking for 1965, supplemented with average figures from the Ministry of Transport returns, and the second set are based on Leicester City 1966 costs as in Table 25.

It would seem reasonable to argue that if a whole route were abandoned, costs of at least level C ought normally to be escaped. Except for Sunday working there were very few City routes which were operating for a revenue which was clearly below this level of cost. For the Midland Red routes, however, 22 out of 91 routes failed to provide revenue to meet the lowest estimate of C level costs while 58 out of 91 routes did not yield enough revenue to meet the highest level (*i.e.*, that applying to the City undertaking). This wide gap between the two estimated cost levels allows not only for uncertainty about appropriate cost levels but also for the uncertain relationship between the revenue level of the day analysed and the yearly average.

An analysis of trip revenue was possible only for Midland Red routes. The whole of the routes operating from Leicester for one day, Tuesday, 29 March 1966, have been analysed and totals only taken for other weekdays in order to be able to make an estimate of day to day fluctuations. These trip revenue figures are shown in Table 27 analysed according to four basic cost levels.

Table 27. Trip revenue on Midland Red routes running to or from Leicester, 29 March 1966

Garage	Revenue per vehicle mile (*d.*)				
	Less than 6.0	6.0–23.9	24.0–37.9	38.0+	Total
Wigston	2	45	104	219	370
Southgate Street	1	148	165	290	604
Sandacre	13	119	151	203	486
Coalville	0	7	18	19	44
Hinckley	0	20	15	3	38
TOTAL	16	339	453	734	1542

The effect of increasing the cost levels by 10%, 20% and 30% is shown in Tables 28–30.

Table 28. Trips on Midland Red routes where revenue met basic cost levels plus 10%, 29 March 1966

Revenue (*d.*/veh. mile) (All garages)	No. of trips
Less than 6.6	21
6.6 – 26.39	399
26.4 – 41.79	484
41.8 and over	638
TOTAL	1542

Table 29. Trips on Midland Red routes where revenue met basic cost levels plus 20%, 29 March 1966

Revenue (*d.*/veh. mile)	No. of trips
Less than 7.2	24
7.2 – 28.7	488
28.8 – 45.59	482
45.6 and over	548
TOTAL	1542

Table 30. Trips on Midland Red routes where revenue met basic cost levels plus 30%, 29 March 1966

Revenue (*d.*/veh. mile)	No. of trips
Less than 8.8	34
8.8 – 31.1	571
31.2 – 49.3	471
49.4 and over	466
TOTAL	1542

These data represent rearrangements of the trip revenue per mile data according to different cost levels which would be met by the revenue obtained. The 'basic' cost levels represent approximate cost levels required to cover certain categories of cost, if the overall Midland Red cost figures applied to operation in the Leicester area. These levels were somewhat simplified compared with the A to E categories used above. The first level is equivalent to level A, the second to level B (fuel costs etc. plus wages) and the third to E (total costs). These cost levels were then raised by 10%, 20%, and 30% in order to examine the effect of moving towards the level of costs known to apply to City buses operating in Leicester. It is not easy to say which is the most appropriate cost level. Since Tuesday is a non-peak day for traffic, revenue would be relatively low. On the other hand the 'basic' cost levels reflecting average costs for the whole of the Midland Red's area are almost certainly lower than those applying to urban running in Leicester.

Despite these problems, some conclusions can be drawn. Even at the highest estimate for cost level A, very few trips produced insufficient revenue to cover this. But even taking the lowest estimate of fuel costs plus drivers' and conductors' wages, a considerable number of trips were not providing the revenue to meet these costs. The numbers of trips not covering cost level B at the lowest estimate (24.0*d.* per vehicle mile) was 23.0% of the total whereas at the highest estimate (31.2*d.* per vehicle mile) this was increased to 39.2% of the total number of trips recorded. The number of trips yielding sufficient revenue to cover total costs ranged from 47.6% on the lowest estimate (38.0*d.* per vehicle mile) to 30.2% on the highest estimate (49.4*d.* per vehicle mile).

These cost figures can also be analysed in terms of cross-subsidization, but before this is done it is necessary to define this somewhat imprecise term. Cross-subsidization may be said to occur when a non-profit maximizing monopolist with separable markets increases the price in one market (moving away from the breakeven 'average cost equals average revenue' position towards the profit maximizing 'marginal cost equals marginal revenue' position) in order to make good the deficit resulting from selling at a loss in another market. As used here the term may be defined as excluding the involuntary form of what is sometimes called cross-subsidization, when prices are averaged because of the difficulty of allocating joint costs to individual products or services. (This practice is still followed to some extent in charging for the transport of goods.) Nor is it held to be cross-subsidization when the revenue from a unit of output in one market covers only its marginal cost while similar units are sold for more than average cost (where marginal cost is less than average cost) in other markets. Thus a bus trip earning more in revenue than its 'marginal costs' of fuel and extra servicing and tyre wear (and where the crew would remain idle if the bus were not run) is not being cross-subsidized from other trips on the same route which earn a surplus over average costs. The trip which only just covers marginal cost is dependent on other trips being run at other times of the day (if they were not run its marginal cost would be much higher) but is not subsidized by them. Marginal cost covering trips would be provided by profit-maximizing operators. As thus defined cross-subsidization can exist between bus routes, between different trips on the same route at different times of the day (where some trips do not cover marginal cost), between the same route at one day, or one season, and another, and between different sections of the same route. The most important form of cross-subsidization in passenger transport is that between routes, particularly between urban and rural routes, or between urban and rural sections of the same route. This form of cross-subsidization was sanctified by the legislation of 1930, by the Thesiger Committee, and, by implication, in the 1965 Report of the Transport Holding Company.

There is clear evidence, in the cost and revenue figures analysed here, of cross-subsidization between different bus routes. As would be expected, this is much more important for the Midland Red, with its many partly rural routes, than for the City undertaking. If cost level C is taken as equivalent to 'route marginal cost' then there were eight subsidized City routes on the figures for Friday, 24 September 1965, and twelve on those for Saturday, 1 May 1965. For the Midland Red undertaking, as already noted, something between 22 and 58 routes needed subsidization. If it were possible to break down overall route revenue into that relating to different sections of operation, it is likely that there would be found to be cross-subsidization between the urban and rural parts of some routes.

There was little evidence of cross-subsidization between different trips on any one route. Even with the highest estimate of Midland Red costs (Table 30) there were only 34 trips with revenue below the A cost level (the appropriate level where the wages of the crew could not be saved by discontinuing the trip), and these may well have been on routes which needed overall subsidization. It is only in the probably few cases where crew costs could be avoided by omitting trips that cross-subsidization may occur. There were 420 Midland Red trips that did not earn enough revenue to meet cost level B+10% (Table 28).

The revenue position of the City services is very much worse on Sundays than on weekdays, and there was clearly cross-subsidization of Sunday running on the Sunday for which an analysis was made (28 March 1965). Twenty-three routes did not cover cost level B which would seem to be a reasonable estimate of the marginal cost of a single day's operation of a bus route.

The question now arises of the respective costs of car and bus travel, and of how far these costs are reflected in prices. There are various cost levels which might be considered but attention here will be confined to marginal costs less fuel tax, marginal costs including tax, and average total costs. As has already been shown the marginal cost of bus operation will vary from one trip to another but perhaps the most suitable definition of marginal cost for comparison with car operation is 'cost level B' which includes vehicle running costs and the wages of the bus crew. The average figure for local authority undertakings in 1964/65 was 26.7*d.* per mile, of which approximately 3.6*d.* was fuel tax, giving a less-tax figure of approximately 23.1*d.* per vehicle mile. The equivalent (for a petrol consumption of 30 m.p.g.) was approximately 1.2*d.* per vehicle mile (petrol at factor costs=1*s.* 9*d.* per gallon plus 0.5*d.* maintenance). This gives a car to bus cost ratio per vehicle mile of 1:19.25. With an average car occupancy of 1.5 this would mean that a bus would need to carry 29 passengers in order to have lower marginal costs per passenger mile. The inclusion of fuel tax in the measurement of marginal cost makes the situation a little more favourable for buses. The car cost then becomes 2.7*d.* per vehicle mile, and the car to bus cost ratio is approximately 1:10, so that the bus would need to carry at least an average of 16 passengers to have lower marginal costs per passenger mile than a car with a 1.5 rate of occupancy.

The average total cost for buses, if we use the figure for municipal undertakings in 1964/65, was 42.4*d.* per passenger mile. The total cost of operating a car will in practice vary even more than the marginal cost, since variations in depreciation depending upon the type of car will be added to the variations in fuel consumption. But for an average figure relating to 1964/65 the rate of payment made by many firms for car journeys of 6.5*d.* per vehicle mile may be used. This gives a car to bus cost ratio per vehicle mile of 1:6.5 and means that a bus would need to carry ten or more passengers compared with a car average load of 1.5 persons to have lower average costs per passenger mile.

The actual price paid for bus travel varies from one undertaking to another, and in some cases there is a sharp decrease in the mileage rate for longer distances, or a step effect with a constant charge over a mileage range and thus a gaining of several pence to the next mileage range. Birmingham Corporations fares in 1965, for example, had a minimum fare of 4*d.* for all distances up to 1.25 miles then a jump to 7*d.* for the mileage range 2.5–3.74 and a fare of 10*d.* for the range 3.75–4.9 miles. The average distance travelled for 3*d.* for 82 municipal and joint undertakings in 1965 was 0.69 miles with a range from 0.3 miles to 2.2 miles. On municipal undertakings in 1965 the average fare for a journey of one mile was 4.18*d.* and that for a three mile journey was 2.69*d.* and that for a six mile journey was 1.94*d.* If the car 'price' is taken as being equivalent to marginal cost then the estimated average car cost of 2.7*d.* per vehicle is almost exactly equal to the average bus price (per passenger mile) for a three mile journey. With a car occupancy of 1.5 persons car travel would actually be cheaper than bus travel (1.8*d.* per passenger mile by car compared with 2.7*d.* by bus).

This comparison is 'unfair' to the buses in that it compares a price based on average cost with the marginal cost of car operation. It seems very probable, however, that this is the way the situation presents itself to most consumers. Almost certainly the majority of 'one car' families would argue that they would need a car for social and other travel even if it was not required for the work journey and that the computation of marginal rather than average costs to the journey to work is therefore justified. It is, however, interesting to compare the bus/car price levels for average car costs. In the case of a car with a single occupant and an average cost of 9*d.* per mile, then the car to bus price ratio for a three mile journey would still be only 1:3.3. A car with four occupants would still have a lower 'price' per passenger mile even using a relatively high average cost figure as the car price basis.

If bus prices were based on marginal cost then they would of course work out below car marginal cost prices in peak periods. With a bus occupancy of 40 and a car occupancy of 1.5 the average prices would be 0.67*d.* per passenger mile and 1.8*d.* per passenger mile respectively. But marginal cost pricing of this form would cause bus undertakings to lose considerable sums (about 15*d.* per vehicle mile) and would only be made possible by large-scale subsidization. Bus fares could probably be reduced in peak periods and increased in off-peak periods without incurring losses though the extent to which this was possible would depend on the demand elasticities of the peak and off-peak periods. The average cost per passenger mile for municipal buses with an occupancy of 40 would be 1.06*d.* so that the average fare of 2.7*d.* per passenger mile could be said to involve a subsidization of non-peak services. On the other hand, as it has already been argued, the marginal cost of peak services is considerably higher than that of off-peak services so that consideration of average or marginal costs gives conflicting results in the relative pricing of peak and off-peak traffic. The higher fares needed to cross-subsidize low density routes by undertakings operating both urban and rural services will clearly tend to distort the choice between cars and buses on urban routes (and, in the opposite way, on rural routes).

In recent years the bus/car price ratio has become increasingly relatively more favourable to the car. Table 31 shows the total expenditure on passenger transport for 1954, 1964 and 1965.

Table 31. Consumers' expenditure on passenger transport[1]

Year	Expenditure (£ million)		Passenger miles ('000 million)		Expenditure per passenger mile (*d.*)		Bus/car expenditure ratio (*d.* per passenger mile)
	Bus	Car	Bus	Car	Bus	Car	
1954	259	425	50.0	47.2	1.24	2.16	1:1.74
1964	360	1605	40.3	125.5	2.14	3.07	1:1.43
1965	369	1708	37.6	134.8	2.35	3.04	1:1.29

[1]*National Income and Expenditure*, 1965, and *Passenger Transport in Great Britain*, 1964 and 1965.

There are certain statistical difficulties involved in these figures. The motoring expenditure is that for purchases of vehicles and running costs and there is an uncertain relationship between depreciation and the costs of purchases in a particular year. The expenditure figures exclude expenditure by companies and public authorities but the passenger mileage estimates are for total passenger transport. Motor expenditure per passenger mile is therefore probably an underestimate, and would in any case be higher for peak urban travel when the car occupancy rate would be lower. But while these factors may cast doubt on the figures of expenditure for car transport there is no reason to believe that they invalidate the conclusion that the 'cost' gap between bus and car travel has been narrowing. This is supported by other figures. The index of bus stage services (with 1953=100) was 102 in 1954, 168 in 1964 and 176 in 1965. The equivalent figures for car prices (new and secondhand) were 100 in 1954 and 94 in both 1964 and 1965. The index of car running costs (with the same base year) was 99 in 1954, 118 in 1964 and 127 in 1965. (The index for rail fares with 1953=100 was 1954=101, 1964=174, 1965=186*.)

This relative increase in the cost of public transport is almost certainly mainly a reflection of increased labour costs. The wages of bus crews alone make up about 74% of the 'marginal cost' of cost level B and about 48% of total operating costs. These costs have increased with rising wages and have also been affected by congestion which leads to poorer vehicle and bus crew utilization. Labour costs are a negligible part of car marginal costs and only a relatively small percentage of total average costs. Car operating costs do not reflect directly the increased demand for scarce urban road space. The quality of service provided by cars has declined when congestion has worsened and journey times have been lengthened, but this applies equally to bus services. It must be concluded therefore that the present pricing system for urban passenger transport has tended to encourage the movement from public to private transport in recent years.

* *Passenger Transport in Great Britain*, 1964 and 1965.

4

The boundary system

The introduction of licensing controls by the Road Traffic Act of 1930 has resulted in the bus industry in Britain becoming organized into a number of local monopolies. The Act made it necessary to obtain a road service licence before any regular bus service can be operated. These licences are granted by the Traffic Commissioners in each of the eleven traffic areas into which the country is divided. The Traffic Commissioners are appointed by the Minister of Transport from a panel of names drawn up by two groups of local authorities. In considering applications for licences the Commissioners have to take into account the suitability of the proposed routes; existing provisions for services on the proposed route; the public interest; and '. . . the needs of the area as a whole in relation to traffic (including the provision of adequately suitable and efficient services, the elimination of unnecessary services and the provision of unremunerative services) and the co-ordination of all forms of passenger transport including transport by rail.'* The effect of this legislation as interpreted by the Commissioners has been to preserve the monopoly or near-monopoly of existing bus undertakings. This means that a problem has developed about the boundaries of the areas of operation of different bus undertakings. In most large towns in Britain the bus service is operated by the municipality. Outside the large cities the bus services may be operated by companies, as is the case in Birmingham and Leicester, or by other local authorities as is common in the southeast Lancashire conurbation. But passenger flows do not by any means conform to boundaries which may have developed mainly by historical accident. In particular in the larger cities and conurbations there are often continuously built up areas where the bus service is divided between a number of different undertakings and where some of the major traffic flows are across the boundaries of bus undertakings.

The 'boundary system' has been justified mainly as part of the whole system designed to make possible the provision of bus services on low-

* Road Traffic Act, 1960, 8 & 9. Eliz. 2 c. 16. Sec. 135 (d). This Act re-enacted the provisions of the 1930 Act with other regulations.

density 'unremunerative' routes. In this chapter the way the present boundary system has developed in Leicester is examined, and its effects on bus operation considered, while its possible justification for 'external' reasons such as the need to cross-subsidize rural services is discussed later.

There are two ways in which it is possible that the boundaries system might have a harmful effect on bus operation. These are that a poorer quality service might result for urban bus passengers, or that the services provided might be more wasteful of resources than they would be if provided by a single undertaking.

The operation of bus routes in Leicester was the subject of one of the first major disputes after the institution of the licensing system in 1930. The Midland Red organization successfully sought variation of a restriction imposed by the East Midlands Traffic Commissioners on the services which they were licensed to operate in Leicester. This restriction forbade them to 'pick up or set down the same passenger or passengers within the City boundary' or within 440 yards of any point on any road 'traversed or used by a service of the Corporation.' The Minister ordered the Commissioners to relax the restriction by removing the prohibition on picking up and setting down within the City boundary, though the 440 yards limitation was retained.*

There are still considerable areas inside the city boundaries where Midland Red hold the licence to operate. The boundaries between the City and Midland Red areas are denoted by 'area stop signs' placed on all the main routes out of the city centre. Since that time there has been some co-operation between the two undertakings in making agreements for operating buses in each other's areas, but this has been very limited. The present situation is shown in Figure 2. The red routes are those where Midland Red operates exclusively. Many of these are well inside the city boundary, such, for example, as those in the Scraptoft, Braunstone and Anstey Lane areas. The green routes are those on which only City buses run. Red/green routes, which are labelled 'dual' routes on the map, are also City routes, but on roads along which Midland Red buses also run. But the Midland Red buses cannot pick up passengers at all on inward journeys, whilst on outward journeys some picking up is permitted, but minimum fares generally apply. The Midland Red stops on these routes are separate from the City stops, though in some cases they are near enough for passengers waiting for a City bus to transfer to a

* Birmingham and Midland Motor Omnibus Co. Ltd. re Leicester Corporation. R.V. 12454, October 1931.

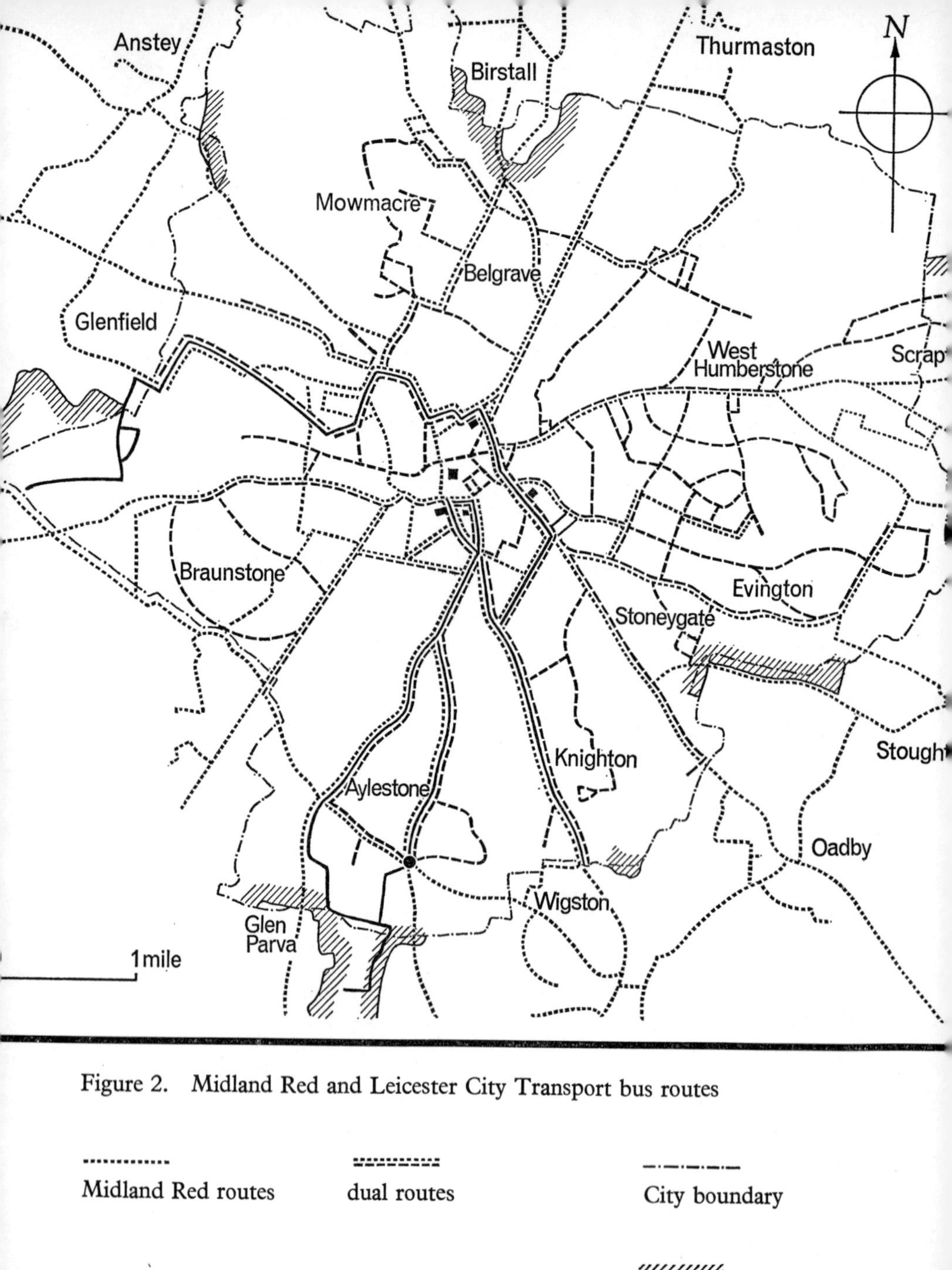

Figure 2. Midland Red and Leicester City Transport bus routes

Midland Red one. (It is unlikely that passengers will wait at a Midland Red stop if they are travelling to a destination served by a City service.) The black lines represent routes which are coordinated. On these routes there are joint bus stops, with equal rights of picking up and putting down, and City and Midland Red buses run in agreed proportions. There are no examples of jointly operated routes, with pooled receipts, in the Leicester area.

In order to investigate the existing situation in Leicester in more detail, two 'case studies' of operations on existing routes have been made. In each case some comparison has been attempted between the present dual operation and a hypothetical service provided by one undertaking.

The first route examined was that along the A6 from the city centre to Oadby. The almost continually built up area on this route extends nearly as far south as the border between Oadby and Great Glen, to a distance of 4.25 miles. The first 2.6 miles of this route are in the service area of the City undertaking and the other 1.6 miles are served by the Midland Red. In this case the boundary coincides with that of the city.

The existing situation on this route may be analysed by taking two bus boarding points which serve different parts of Oadby. These are the junction of Ash Tree Road with the A6 (Glen Road) and Oadby Church, which is in the centre of the town. The total number of buses serving Ash Tree Road on a Friday was 53 plus 23 buses (on route L86) stopping so near Ash Tree Road that they can be counted in, giving a total of 76 outward buses. (With some very minor exceptions there were the same number of inward buses as

Table 32. Arrival of buses bound for central Leicester at Oadby Church bus stop, morning peak period, Fridays

Time	Nature of service (Urban or Rural)	Time	Nature of service (Urban or Rural)
7.20	Rural	8.10	Urban
7.22	Urban	8.15	Urban
7.28	Rural	8.25	Urban
7.30	Rural	8.35	Rural
7.38	Urban	8.35	Rural
7.40	Urban	8.40	Urban
7.55	Urban	9.05	Urban
7.55	Rural	9.15	Urban
8.05	Urban		

outward buses for both the stopping points examined.) Of these buses 34 served only Oadby, the rest going out into the country (10 of them only as far as Great Glen, which is a borderline 'urban' service). There were 81 buses going out to Oadby Church by a direct route, and another 12 which served it but by a roundabout route. Of these 81, 50 were urban services serving Oadby (30 of these made a circular trip via Wigston), and the other 31 also served country areas. All but 25 of the Ash Tree Road buses also stopped at Oadby Church, and have therefore been counted in both totals. The total number of buses serving different parts of Oadby by a direct route was 106. But these were not spread out evenly in time, and the arrival of some buses at the same stop at very close intervals must considerably reduce their effectiveness. The actual arrival of buses going to Leicester at Oadby Church bus stop is shown in Table 32.

Six of these buses were timetabled to arrive within two minutes of another bus (three of them at the same time) so that they did little to shorten the gaps between buses on the timetable, and the average number of passengers picked up must be small. This situation is, of course, largely unavoidable with buses converging from several different rural areas, but it does mean that most of the rural buses can make little contribution to the carriage of passengers from Oadby into Leicester during peak periods. On the other hand, some degree of 'bunching' of bus times may be desirable where passengers do not arrive randomly at bus stops.

The fare on all buses from central Leicester to Ash Tree Road, or *vice versa* (except two minimum fare buses originating from Saddington) was 1*s*. 4*d*. That from or to Oadby Church was 1*s*. 1*d*.

Midland Red buses coming out from Leicester pick up and drop passengers at stops which are distinct from, though generally near to, the City Transport stops. There is a minimum fare from central Leicester of 8*d*. but this does not apply to passengers picked up at Victoria Park Gates or beyond. On the inwards journey there is a minimum fare of 8*d*. from Glebe Road (the last stop before the City boundary) to any stopping place in the City. Midland Red buses do not pick up passengers at all in the City area on inward journeys.

The Leicester City bus service to the city boundary along London Road (turning off just before the boundary at Shanklin Drive) provides 118 bus journeys in each direction on a Friday (as on Monday to Thursday), regularly spaced between each hour, but with some increase of frequency at peak periods. The interesting question now arises of how the existing service provided by the Midland Red to people in Oadby would compare with that which would be provided by extending the City Transport route 29 to Oadby Church and Ash Tree Road. It must first be made clear, however, that what is being compared is the kind of service which might have been expected to develop if a single undertaking had been responsible for all bus routes running to the southern borders of Oadby. This has nothing to do with the relative merits of the City and Midland Red type of organization but attempts to compare the results of dividing the whole route between two undertakings with single undertaking operation. Whether the single undertaking was organized as a company or as a local authority is assumed to be irrelevant.

The main points of comparison, in so far as they would affect passengers to or from Oadby, are set out in Table 33.

Table 33. Present and hypothetical services from Leicester to Oadby Church

Present service	Hypothetical City Service
81 direct buses	118 direct buses
Timetabling irregular	Timetabling regular
12 non-direct routes	None
25 serving other parts of Oadby	None
Fare 1*s.* 1*d.*	Fare 7*d.*–8*d.*
Picking up on outward route in City, minimum fare from centre	Picking up on outward route, no minimum fare
Minimum fare from outside boundary	No minimum fare
Quicker inward journeys on unfilled buses	Slower inward journeys on unfilled buses

There can be little doubt that on balance the hypothetical extended City route would provide the superior service, though there would be both gains and losses involved. The advantages of extending a City type service do not come mainly from the total number of buses provided. There were in all exactly the same number of Midland Red buses serving some part of Oadby (counting those using an indirect route) in each direction (118) as there were City buses running to the boundary. Running all 118 bus journeys to Oadby Church would make the service poorer to other parts of Oadby and it is impossible to say whether or not the gains to the users of stops in the centre of the town would be offset by the losses to those in the more outlying areas. But the irregular timetabling of the Midland Red routes reduces their effectiveness, the difference in fare of 38–46% must be significant,* and the minimum fare and picking up restrictions are serious disadvantages for Oadby travellers

* The fare for the hypothetical extended City route was estimated by a simple extension of the mileage rate at present applying on the 29 route.

not going to or from the City centre. The effects on passengers travelling entirely within the City is not shown in Table 34. If the existing 118 bus journeys were simply extended to Oadby then City travellers would, of course, lose by having some buses arrive already full, and by a disturbance of the timetabling (with the loss of either the earliest inward journeys or the latest outward journey in exchange for additional late inward or early outward journeys). The number of buses operating on the route would clearly have to be increased. This raises the issue of how a single undertaking would compare with divided control of the route in making the best use of scarce resources. (Again it is the efficiency of one compared with that of two operators for a given length of urban route, rather than the advantages of different types of management that is under consideration.) This is a complicated problem which is worthy of a complete study of its own. If a simple extension of the present City bus service is considered, then an approximate tally of gains and losses can be made. The City service would have to operate more buses to keep up the same quality of service in the existing City area. They would need to supplement the service in peak periods in order to be able to carry the City area passengers, and extra buses would be needed if neither the early inward nor the late outward trips were to be sacrificed. Wage, fuel and maintenance costs would increase in correspondence with the extra bus mileage run. On the other hand all the 'urban' Midland Red buses would no longer need to run except that half of the 30 circular bus journeys (L10) would still be needed to run to Wigston. This would provide a saving of approximately 71 bus journeys.* It is assumed that the country buses would run as before, continuing any contribution that they make at present to carrying passengers from Oadby, and possibly also, from stops inside the City area as well where timetabling made this worth while. If a single undertaking could provide a service as good as that now given on the City route 29, to Ash Tree Road, Oadby, at a cost of 71 extra bus journeys or less, then this would be an improvement on the present situation. If it took more than 71 extra bus journeys to achieve this, then it would be necessary to compare the cost of the extra journeys with the benefits received from the improved service. The number of passengers actually picked up in Oadby between 71.5 and 9.15 A.M. (on 29 March 1966) was 472. A ten minute service of buses with a capacity of 70 would provide 840 seats in a two-hour period.

* This is counting the Great Glen route as 'urban' but assumes that Great Glen passengers would be able to be accommodated on existing 'rural buses' passing through that village.

The most obvious inefficiency resulting from the present division of the service to Oadby between two undertakings is the unused bus seat capacity on the Midland Red buses on the inwards journey inside the City undertaking's area. Table 34 shows the number of empty seats on Midland Red buses during the morning peak period on the two days analysed.

Table 34. Minimum number of empty seats available on buses through Oadby forbidden to pick up inside Leicester, 7.15–9.15 A.M.

Route	No. of buses	No. of buses with a peak load > 70 pass.	Minimum number of empty seats
Tuesday, 29 *March* 1966			
L.10	5	0	203
L11	3	0	173
L32	4	0	113
L86	4	0	154
611	1	0	36
639	3	0[1]	75
Friday, 8 *April* 1966			
L10	6	0	313
L11	2	0	118
L32	4	0	204
L82	2	0	118
L86	4	0	234
611	2	0	68
639	3	0[2]	119
615	1	0	57

[1]Including one single-decker with a peak load of 44; [2]including one single-decker with a peak load of 34.

The number of seats empty is described as the 'minimum' number because the estimate was obtained by taking the peak loading figure at any stage away from the assumed bus capacities but some of these people may have got off before the City boundary was crossed. Low figures for bus capacities of 70 for a double-decker bus and 45 for a single-decker bus were used. The times used (generally those for the Oadby bus stop used by that route which was the most distant from Leicester) were those actually recorded on the waybills, and were not necessarily identical with the timetable times shown in Table 32.

The figures show that there was considerable spare seat capacity on Midland Red buses running along 2.6 miles of densely populated route into central Leicester which could not be used because of the present licensing system. On the conservative estimates of bus capacity used here and even on the day with the heavier flow of passengers, this represented 54.8% of the total bus capacity. The sterilization of this capacity seems to be a high price to pay in order to make it possible to cross-subsidize country routes or so that Oadby passengers can have a quicker run into Leicester than a stopping bus would provide. (Though Midland Red buses can, and do, stop to set down inside the City area.)

The second route analysed in detail was that to Birstall, a built-up area north of the City boundary. The City boundary was 2.6 miles from the City centre and the northern edge of Birstall was 3.6 miles from central Leicester. The City bus service (40) ran via Belgrave Road and Loughborough Road to a point near the Leicester boundary, then ran back towards the City for about half a mile down Abbey Lane to its terminal at the junction with Thurcaston Road. The inward journey covered the same route in reverse. Midland Red ran three 'country' routes (625, 627, 628) out along the main road (Loughborough Road) running through Birstall, and mostly terminating at Loughborough, though a few ran on to Derby. Another Loughborough bus (626) took a similar route except for running on the 'loop' route (which can be distinguished on Figure 2) via Birstall Road and Sibsons Road, rejoining Loughborough Road at Sibsons Corner. The 625 and 626 routes were coordinated with the Trent Motor Traction Company. There were 18 outward Trent buses out of a total of 80 on the four services 625–628 on a weekday. There were three urban Midland Red routes serving Birstall. The L40 ran along the Loughborough Road as far as Sibsons Road Corner, then turning off to serve the built-up area to the east of Loughborough Road, while the L85 ran to the same point but turned off to serve the area to the west of Loughborough Road. The L30 followed the same loop route as 626 but did not rejoin the Loughborough Road, terminating at the same point as L40. The last inward picking up point on all routes was the Hotel Belgrave (Loughborough Road, Leicester) except for 627 when it was in Abbey Lane. The minimum outwards fare on all routes was *6d.* The total number of outwards Midland Red buses serving the Birstall area was 157 and the corresponding inwards total was 163. The arrival of inwards buses during the period 7.15–9.15 A.M. at Sibsons Road Corner is shown in Table 35.

Table 35. Arrival of buses bound for central Leicester at Sibsons Road Corner, Birstall, Friday, 7.15–9.15 A.M.

Time	Nature of service (Urban or Rural)
7.15	Rural
7.18	Urban
7.19	Urban
7.22	Rural
7.25	Rural
7.32	Urban
7.32	Rural
7.35	Rural
7.41	Urban
7.42	Urban
7.42	Rural
7.45	Rural
7.47	Rural
7.50	Rural
7.55	Rural
8.01	Urban
8.02	Rural
8.04	Urban
8.12	Rural
8.17	Urban
8.22	Rural
8.26	Urban
8.32	Rural
8.34	Urban
8.35	Rural
8.37	Rural
8.38	Urban
8.45	Urban
8.52	Rural
9.02	Rural
9.07	Urban
9.12	Rural

The maximum gap between buses between 8.00 and 9.00 A.M. was 8 minutes, and the average frequency was 3.9 minutes, though in some cases the 'bunching' was so close that some buses would be ineffective for Sibsons Road Corners passengers. Not all these buses took the same route inward to the city centre but all eventually ran to St Margarets or The Newarke bus stations. The City undertaking ran 118 buses out to Thurcaston Road, evenly spaced between hours and with maximum frequency at peak periods. The existing Midland Red service is compared with a hypothetical extension of the City service, in the same manner as the Oadby comparison, in Table 36.

Table 36. Present and hypothetical services from Leicester to Sibsons Road Corner, weekdays

Present service	Hypothetical service
135 direct or semi-direct buses	118 direct buses
Timetabling irregular	Timetabling regular
22 serving other parts of Birstall	None
Peak frequency 14 per hour	Peak frequency 9 per hour
Fare 11*d.*	Fare 10*d.*
Picking up on outward route, minimum fare 6*d.*	Picking up everywhere, no minimum fare
No inward picking up inside city boundary	
Quicker inward journeys on unfilled buses	Slower inward journeys on unfilled buses

This comparison provides a contrast with the Oadby one. Birstall travellers are clearly getting as good a service as they would be likely to receive from a single undertaking. There appear to be several reasons for this. The geography of Birstall is different and buses can follow the loop road and return to the central road, or diverge to outlying estates after traversing most of the central route. The different buses serving Oadby do not all run through the main part of the built-up area. Probably more important, the 'country' buses at Birstall run out through more densely populated country than that south of Oadby, and terminate at Loughborough, not at country villages. A more frequent 'rural' or long distance service can thus be justified. On the evidence of the traffic figures studied Birstall would appear to have more buses than the demand warrants. Thus the total number of passengers picked up by Midland Red buses in Birstall between 7.15 and 9.15 A.M. on the busier of the two days studied (29 March 1966) was 831. During this two-hour period 28 buses were timetabled to stop at Sibsons Road Corner on journeys into Leicester (there were also four operated by Trent Motor Traction Co., whose passengers were not included in the total of 831). The country buses carried another 114 passengers from beyond Birstall. The overall load factor was therefore 48.2% on an average bus capacity of 70 (or 45.0% on a bus capacity of 75). It would seem likely that this could be improved by reducing the number of buses though this would depend, of course, on the sensitivity of demand to relatively small changes in bus timetabling.

Where the present system is clearly wasteful, as was also found in the Oadby case study, is in failing to use the empty seats available on Midland Red buses inside the Leicester City area. Table 37 shows the position on buses coming into the city through Birstall. The number of empty seats was calculated as with the Oadby comparison, using a capacity figure of 70.

Table 37. Minimum number of empty seats available on buses through Birstall forbidden to pick up inside Leicester, 7.15–9.15 A.M.

Route	No. of buses	No. of buses with a peak load of >70 passengers	Minimum number of empty seats
Tuesday, 29 *March* 1966			
L40	12	2	332
L85	4	1	123
625–8[1]	12	0	577
Friday, 8 *April* 1966			
L40	13	0	524
L85	3	0	125
625–8[1]	13	0	681

[1]Excludes Trent Motor Traction Co. buses.

It should therefore be possible to reduce the number of bus journeys made by the City services if even a proportion of these seats could be used.

It has been suggested in the two detailed studies of routes running from central Leicester that division of the route between two undertakings has led to an inferior service being provided in one case, and in both cases to a wasteful use of resources. The issue of how far such a 'dual' operation of a service must be inherently inefficient may now be examined more generally and theoretically. The problem can be examined by taking a simplified situation with a regular and predictable flow of passengers where the optimum strategy for a bus undertaking can easily be determined. Suppose that on a route with equally spread stops numbered 1 to n, where n was the most distant from the city centre, there was an inward flow of x passengers per a minutes, where a was the frequency of the bus service and b was the capacity of each bus. It is assumed that x is a function of the bus frequency which is maximized at a, and that the object of the bus undertaking strategy is to maximize the bus load factor on the inward journey. The best strategy would then be to have one ten-minute bus service serving all stops from n up to and including $(n+1)-\frac{b}{x}$ and another service picking up passengers at the remaining $n-\frac{b}{x}$ stops.* For example, if there were ten stops with a required bus frequency of ten minutes, and fifteen passengers per ten minutes period at each stop, with a bus capacity of 75 then the first bus route should go from stop 10 to stop 6 and the second from stop 5 to stop 1. If $x=10$, the other figures remaining the same, the first bus route would run from stop 10 to stop 4, the second from stop 3 to stop 1. Now the optimum strategy would only be open to a bus undertaking operating a dual system if the boundary happened to be at the right point on the route. Thus if the route with 15 passengers per 10 minutes was divided at the optimum point, between stop 5 and 6 the number of buses required for the furthest leg of the route, if the total running time from the centre to n and back (including any terminal time) was 60 minutes would be $\frac{60}{10}=6$. For the service from stop 5, with a total running time of 30 minutes $\frac{30}{10}=3$ buses would be required, a total of 9 buses. But if the boundary on a dual system happened to lie between stops 7 and 6 then the first route from stops 10 to 7 would still require 6 buses. The route from stop 6 to stop 2 would (assuming an extra 3 minutes running time) require $\frac{33}{10}=4$ buses.† Another bus would also be required to serve stop 1, so that the new total number of buses needed would be $6+4+1=11$. Real life timetabling and routing problems are very much more complex than this, but the complications only tend to make it more unlikely that the pattern of operation obtainable by two undertakings on a route with an arbitrarily imposed boundary will approximate as closely to the optimum as that which a single undertaking could obtain when free from artificial boundary restrictions. These real life complications include an irregular, unpredictable demand for bus transport, various peaks in demand, interrelationships between frequency of service and demand and between the number of stops made and running time, and the effect of varying congestion conditions on

* If $x(n-\frac{b}{x})>b$, a further division of the route would be necessary.

† If the frequency of a route $=F$ and the total journey time, including stops and terminal time, is T then the number of buses required is $\frac{T}{F}$, any fraction being taken as a whole number.

running times. They are all factors which will change quite quickly so that the best strategy for a bus undertaking to follow will change also, and the present boundary system must make change more difficult.

The present boundary system must then, be held to be a barrier in the way of obtaining improved operational efficiency. It might indeed be argued that the present licensing system has resulted in one of the worst possible systems of boundaries in towns like Leicester. If Leicester had to be divided for urban bus transport then a north/south or east/west division, whereby one undertaking could control the whole length of an urban route from the centre outwards, would be preferable to a system which divides the inner from the outer suburbs.

There are many towns in which the artificial barriers imposed by the licensing system have been overcome far more effectively than in Leicester. It would be interesting to compare bus operation in a city like Sheffield, where there is widespread joint operation, with that in Leicester. But the possibility that a disadvantage can be overcome (usually at the cost of considerable time and after the expenditure of much administrative skill) need not stop us asking whether the disadvantage itself could not be removed.

In the Oadby case study one issue that arose was the choice between a single and more frequent service through the centre of a suburban area; and the division of the last part of the route to run through different parts of the suburb at less frequent intervals. This is another issue which may be considered more generally.

The optimum strategy for routing buses will depend on the chosen objectives and the assumptions made about the behaviour of prospective passengers. It is perhaps one of the major disadvantages of the present organization of the bus system that undertakings have no clear cut, easily recognizable objectives. Profit maximization (or loss minimization), sales maximization, and various ill-defined social obligations may all be possible objectives for a bus undertaking. For the purpose of considering routing, limited but definite objectives may be laid down. Let us assume, in the first place, that the objective is to minimize passengers' walking time, and that there is an area from which passengers originate which can be divided into three non-intersecting zones in each of which travelling time to a possible bus stop is two minutes, arranged as shown in Figure 3.

Figure 3. Bus routing model

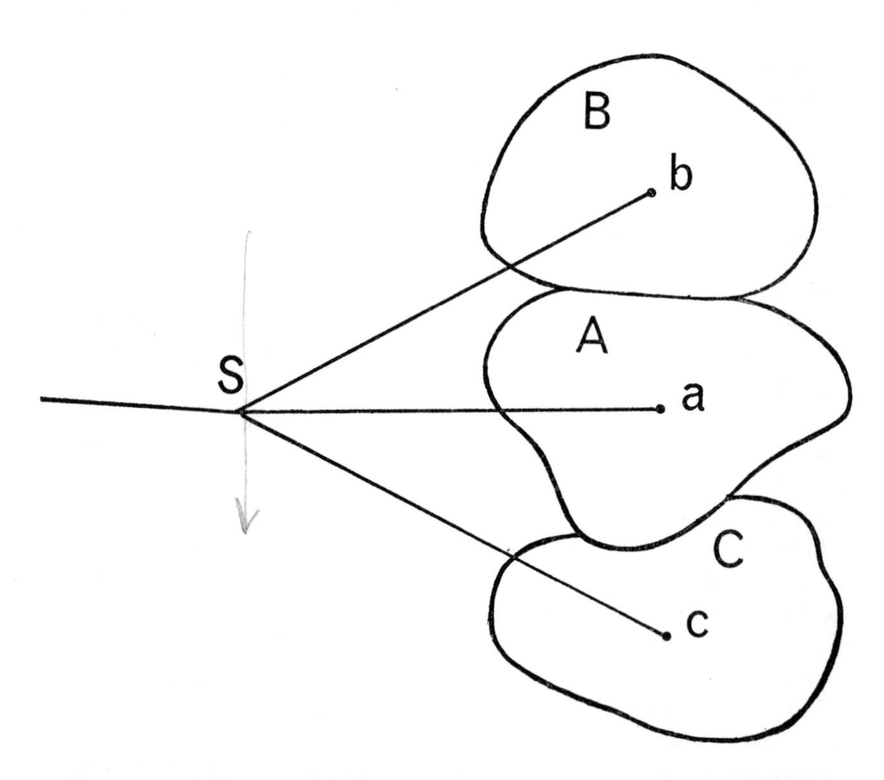

Let it be further assumed that it is intended to run one bus every ten minutes to serve the area, and that each zone generates three passengers per minute or thirty per ten-minute period. Then the choice is between sending a bus to a every ten minutes, or splitting the route at S and sending buses to a, b and c alternately. Now if we are concerned with passengers travelling to work then it seems reasonable to assume that they must arrive at work at fixed times. There will therefore be a number of passengers for whom each bus is the latest possible bus for getting to work on time. For simplicity of exposition it may be assumed that 30 passengers from each zone must catch buses departing for the City centre not later than 8.10 A.M., and the same number must travel at 8.20 and 8.30. (It is assumed that the journey time from a, b and c are all the same.) This means that passengers living in one zone must be prepared to walk to the bus stop in another zone if that is where their 'latest bus' leaves from. Now the average walking times in minutes from any zone to any stop may be estimated to be approximately as shown in the following matrix:

Zone/Bus stop	a	b	c
A	2	10	10
B	10	2	20
C	10	20	2

If the average travelling time to the centrally placed bus stop in each zone was two minutes then the boundaries would be about five minutes away (there is no need to assume a perfectly circular zone or passengers originating exactly evenly throughout the zone, though for the later argument it is convenient to assume that the concentration of potential passengers is equal in both halves of any zone divided by a line through the central bus stop and parallel to the boundary which touches that of the next zone). Then the average travelling time to the zone border would be five minutes and it would take ten minutes for zone B and zone C dwellers to cross zone A.

The first alternative would be to send a bus to start its inward journey from a at 8.10, another to leave b at 8.20, and the third to leave c at 8.30. This would give a total walking time (T_1) if the total passengers from A, B and C for each ten-minute period are represented by P_A, P_B and P_C respectively, as in the equation below.

$$T_1 = 22P_A + 32P_B + 32P_C$$

The clearly superior alternative is to send all buses to stop a, when the total walking time (T_2) of passengers would be as in the next equation.

$$T_2 = 6P_A + 30P_B + 30P_C$$

This shows that even if the assumption of equal passenger generation in each zone is dropped the second situation, where all buses go to the single stop a, will yield the lower total passenger walking time. This must be true for any values of P_A, P_B and P_C since all the coefficients are smaller in the second equation. This does not, of course, mean that sending all buses to a would be the walking-time minimizing solution for any values of P_A, P_B and

P_C. If the passenger generation of one zone other than A increases it will eventually be better to route buses into this zone. This point can be easily calculated given the walking times and traffic generation of each zone. Suppose that walking times remained as in the model but the traffic generation of zone c was known to have increased greatly and a choice had to be made between sending two buses to c and one to a or continuing to send all buses to a. The breakeven point would come where

$$22P_A+50P_B+14P_C=6P_A+30P_B+30P_C$$

or

$$16P_A+20P_B=16P_C$$

Where, as in the original model, $P_A=P_B$ then it would reduce total travelling time by sending two buses to c and one to a so long as

$$\frac{P_A}{P_C}>\frac{16}{36}$$

or whenever the generation of traffic in C became greater than that in A by a ratio of more than 1:2.25.

So far the argument has, however, been based on one very important implicit assumption which is certainly not true in the current experience of bus undertakings. This is that although passengers will be lost if a bus is not provided for them at the right time for their work journey, their use of buses will not be affected by the length of the walk to the bus stop. Now although the equations of the walking-time minimization model show that (with equal traffic generation in each zone) routing all buses to a gives the best solution for travellers as a whole, some people will be worse off compared with the a b c routing. For example those living in zone C and having to catch the 8.30 will have an average walk of ten minutes instead of their two minutes average walk if the 8.30 was routed to c instead of a. But it is a reasonable assumption that there will be a maximum walking time which people will accept for work journeys by bus; if the journey takes longer than this they will travel by car. Bus undertakings seeking to find the maximum revenue per route mile may then have the important restraint imposed on their route planning that passengers must not be asked to walk for more than a given number of minutes. If the assumptions of the walking time minimization model are retained, but the objective is changed to that of maximization of passengers carried, and a maximum acceptable walking time constraint is added, then the results would be as shown in the two matrices below.

A. Passengers carried. Maximum walking time=5 minutes

	a	b	c
A	30	0	0
B	0	30	0
C	0	0	30

B. Passengers carried. Maximum walking time=10 minutes

	a	b	c
A	30	15	15
B	15	30	0
C	15	0	30

The figures of fifteen for Ab, Ac, Ba and Ca in matrix B were based on the assumption that half of zone A would be able to walk to b and the other half to c in ten minutes and that half of each of zones B and C could reach a in the given maximum walking time. The results show that with a maximum walking time of five minutes or less (and with the given resources of only one bus every ten minutes) then the total flow of passengers will be the same whether all buses go to a or alternate buses to a, b and c. With a maximum walking time of ten minutes, passenger flow is maximized by sending all buses to a. This will remain true for any maximum walking distance greater than five minutes and less than 25 minutes (when all passengers could reach any bus stop).* This conclusion, that it will be at least as good, and usually better, if passenger flow is to be maximized, to concentrate buses on a single individual route, given conditions approximating to those in the model, may seem surprising as it means partly ignoring areas of equal importance as a source of traffic. It depends critically on the assumption that passengers must catch specific buses or be late for work. If this is dropped, and it is assumed that all the potential passengers from each zone would be prepared to travel by the latest bus, then the situation is quite different. If passengers were 'generated' randomly in each zone of the model at the rate of three per

* A walking time as long as 25 minutes for everyone is unlikely on the assumptions of the model since some passengers would be better off if they caught an earlier bus than required from their own 'zonal' bus stop. Thus if the bus inward journey departures were timetabled at a 8.10; b 8.20; c 8.30 then travellers living on the extremities of zone B who would reach work in time on the 8.30 from c would do better to catch the 8.20 from b. For the former they would have to leave home at 8.15 for the latter at 8.05.

minute throughout the 30-minute period then passengers who could be carried are as shown below. (It is assumed that there is no flow of passengers between zones, *i.e.*, maximum acceptable walking time is less than five minutes.)

Passengers available. All departure times acceptable

	a	b	c
A	30	0	0
B	0	60	0
C	0	0	90

Sending three buses to a would yield only 30 passengers whereas alternating and starting with a at 8.10 would yield 165 (if the bus capacity was 75). The optimal strategy, if passengers were really indifferent between any departure times up to 8.30 would, of course, be neither of those considered so far, but sending out three buses which would depart from a, b and c at 8.25.* But this assumption seems very unlikely to apply to those travelling to work, though it may be different for shoppers.

Summarizing this discussion it has been shown that if there is a continuous area from which traffic originates with three roads passing through it so that there is a choice between continuing one central route or dividing this into three, then with given bus resources and if some walking between the different zones and the central bus stop is acceptable, then it is more likely to minimize total walking time and maximize passenger flow if all buses are concentrated on the central route during the period of the journey to work. The existence of more than one stop in each zone would complicate the arithmetic of this discussion, but not affect the conclusion.

* Nothing has been said about the rest of the route into the City centre after the three routes to a, b and c joined because it has been assumed that each 'leg' was of equal length, and therefore the service on this part of the route would not be affected, except that the number of passengers already on the bus at the time of the junction would vary. If all buses departed at 8.25 with full loads then the bus undertaking would be making the most efficient possible use of them unless outward traffic flow was of any importance. Whether or not the traffic on the City side of the junction of the a, b and c legs of the route warranted the use of extra buses is a separate question.

5

Criteria for seeking a transfer of passengers from car to bus

Even for those who believe unquestioningly in the idea of consumer sovereignty, that consumers are the best judges of their own interests, and that the government should not interfere in any way with their 'free choice,' there are problems about the consumption of road space. Consumers only exercise a free choice within the framework of the decisions made by governments about road building, about taxation, about the right to park cars, and about the rights of different road users on the roads. The government cannot simply abstain from influencing the choice of travellers between different modes of passenger transport. The present choices made are already strongly influenced by past government policy, – or in some cases lack of policy. Even where the government does nothing this may be a choice-influencing policy. For example there has been a continuous decline in the use of bicycles in Britain in recent years. This is no doubt partly because people have become richer and prefer scooters or motor cycles or cars instead of bicycles. But it is also partly because the 'law of the jungle' applies on the roads in regard to cars and cycles. The growth of motoring has made cycling increasingly dangerous and unattractive, and cycles have been driven off the road, not because of the exercise of consumer sovereignty through the market mechanism, nor because of any policy decision, but because, in the absence of any action at all to preserve the rights of cyclists, cars make road use unpleasant for cyclists while cyclists have relatively little effect on the enjoyment of the roads by car drivers. In the same way buses and cars dispute for urban road space in a way which cannot be settled entirely by the mechanism of the market. Congestion caused by cars on the roads delays bus services and makes them irregular, and this tends to drive more people into transferring into cars, which may worsen congestion, and the position of the buses, still further. The choice open to the government is not between interfering and not interfering with people's choice between cars and buses, it is rather about the way in which government influence should be exerted.

It is clear that an optimum division of traffic between car and bus will not be achieved only by rationalizing the present legal and financial framework imposed on bus undertakings, important as this may be. Public transport in London has been controlled since 1932 by a single undertaking with an area large enough to enable it to be free of most of the restrictions imposed on undertakings in the rest of the country, but this has not solved the issue of the proper division of road space between buses and cars. If government policy is to seek to halt or reverse the drift from bus to car in recent years, then it is important to find some kind of criterion for distinguishing between roads or areas where the present modal split between car and bus is acceptable, and those where it is not. This is the main problem with which this chapter is concerned.

It is a widely accepted claim of transport policy* that the trend from public to private transport ought to be halted or reversed. This, of course, is because buses normally use less road space per passenger than do private cars. In calculations relating speed to the volume of traffic flow a bus is generally estimated to be the equivalent of three 'passenger car units.' With average car loads of approximately 1.5 persons on urban roads in peak periods, this means that any bus with an average load of more than 4.5 passengers is using less road space per passenger than a private car. At this level of loading buses would be less efficient than cars when the other scarce resources of labour and capital equipment are considered (*i.e.*, their total costs per passenger mile would be higher), but at normal peak period loads of about 40 passengers for a double-decker bus they would easily be the more efficient operators. Since urban road space is already generally congested, and as it is extremely unlikely that the supply of extra road space will keep up with the growth in traffic in the next five or ten years, the *prima facie* case for a greater use of buses is very strong. But this leaves out of consideration the very important issue of quality of service. The continued changeover from public to private urban transport in Britain in recent years suggests that the car, even at a higher price, is preferred as a form of transport to the bus. The reasons for this preference may be complex, and may differ for different individuals; but it seems reasonable to assume that as far as the journey to work is concerned the outstandingly

* See for example the discussion in *Transport Policy*, para. 66, Ministry of Transport.

important factor is the length of 'door to door' journey time. In their pioneering study Wardrop and Smeed showed that even in Central London total car journey time averaged only half total bus journey time for distances of three to five miles.*

There are three reasons for the car advantage in total door-to-door journey time. The bus 'terminal' times will consist of the walk from a passenger's house to the bus stop, the wait for the bus, and the walk from the bus stop to the ultimate destination at the other end of the journey. Car terminal times involve getting the car out of the garage at the beginning of the journey and parking it and walking to the destination at the other end. Despite the worsening parking conditions, it is almost certainly true that for most people in most places the bus terminal times remain much longer than car terminal times. Secondly, the 'vehicle journey speed' of the car on the journey will usually be higher than that of a bus. There is, unfortunately, a lack of reliable figures on the difference between bus and car vehicle speeds in relation to congestion levels. Generally it may be expected that the speed advantage of cars will get smaller with increasing congestion, and may eventually disappear altogether. The situation will, of course, vary considerably on different roads according to the number of bus stops per mile and the degree of difficulty involved in overtaking. A third, and usually less important, advantage of cars is that the total door-to-door distance may be shorter than when the journey is made by bus.

If average door-to-door journey time is at present nearly always shorter by car than by bus, then a policy aimed at securing a car-to-bus transfer needs some justification other than that of the superior road utilization obtained from buses. Still higher road utilization could be obtained from the use of Nigerian mammy wagons with 40 people perched in the back of a converted lorry, but they may be supposed to have more than compensating disadvantages. A car-to-bus transfer policy can most easily be justified if it can be shown that it would result in shorter door-to-door journey times for everyone. Suppose that on a uniformly congested road Xb passengers travel by bus and Xc by car, both at a vehicle speed of S miles per hour, that bus passengers' average terminal time is α minutes and that of car passengers is

* R. J. Smeed and J. G. Wardrop, 'An Exploratory Comparison of the Advantages of Cars and Buses for Travel in Urban Areas,' *Institute of Transport Journal*, March 1964. This comparison was itself partly based on a study by E. Holroyd and D. Scraggs of the Road Research Laboratory, now published as 'Journey Times by Car and Bus in Central London,' *Traffic Engineering and Control*, 1964, 6, (3), 1969–173.

β minutes (where $\alpha < \beta$), that the transfer of ΔXc car travellers to buses would result in a speed increase of ΔS m.p.h., and that the average length of journey of both bus and car passengers along the congested road is L miles. Then so long as the savings in vehicle journey time of the transferred travellers $\left[\frac{60L}{S} - \frac{60L}{S+\Delta S}\right]$ is greater than the loss of 'terminal' time $(\alpha - \beta)$ everyone must gain, since both the original bus passengers and the 'continuing' car passengers will have shorter journey times. Now if the supply of road space is assumed to be fixed, and if the present trends of growing car ownership and of bus-to-car passenger transfers are continued into the future, it becomes increasingly likely that the condition described above, that everyone's door-to-door journey time would be reduced by a car-to-bus transfer, will be fulfilled. As the average traffic flow speed (S) becomes smaller the proportionate increase in speed resulting from a reduction in the total traffic flow $\left[\frac{\Delta S}{S}\right]$ is likely to become greater, while the 'terminal' time difference will remain constant. Eventually S would equal zero and any increase in it would be infinitely great.

Given the continuance of present trends, then, a car-to-bus transfer can be justified as a policy objective, on the reasonable grounds that eventually all travellers would enjoy time savings. But there are many congested roads in Britain, probably the great majority, where the condition of universal time savings from an immediate car-to-bus transfer does not yet exist. A more immediately applicable criterion would be to hold that a 'compulsory' transfer is justified where it would result in the reduction of the total door-to-door journey time of all passengers using the road. This 'total journey time' criterion depends upon a value judgment. It cannot be justified by formal welfare criteria, since no allowance is made for different valuations of time savings by different individuals. The 'losers,' if this criterion were applied (leaving aside all questions of compensation by a lower price, and considering only time savings or losses), would be those people who were transferred from car to bus, while 'original' bus passengers and 'continuing' car travellers would gain.

Assuming that only city centre bus or car commuters used the road, retaining for the moment the assumption that buses and cars had the same vehicle speed, using the symbols already introduced, and denoting the pre-transfer total door-to-door journey time in minutes by T_1, this would then be given by

$$T_1 = (X_b + X_c)\frac{60L}{S} + \alpha X_b + \beta X_c$$

and the post-transfer journey time, T_2, would be given by

$$T_2 = (X_b + X_c)\frac{60L}{S + \Delta S} + \alpha(X_b + \Delta X_c) + \beta(X_c - \Delta X_c)$$

The net change in total door-to-door journey time ($T_1 - T_2$) would therefore be

$$T_1 - T_2 = X_b + X_c \left[\frac{60L}{S} - \frac{60L}{S + \Delta S}\right] - \Delta X_c\,(\beta - \alpha)$$

In the rather more complex case where car vehicle speeds are greater than bus vehicle speeds, by an assumed constant i (but where the speed increase from the car-bus transfer is the same absolute amount, ΔS, for both cars and buses) the change in total door-to-door journey time will be given by

$$T_1 - T_2 = X_b \left[\frac{60L}{S} - \frac{60L}{S + \Delta S}\right] + X_c \left[\frac{60L}{S + i + \Delta S}\right] + \Delta X_c \left[\frac{60L}{S + i + \Delta S} - \frac{60L}{S + \Delta S}\right] + \Delta X_c\,(\beta - \alpha)$$

This formula is still simplified in that the bus/car modal split is assumed to be constant over the whole length of the congested road, and all traffic other than commuter cars and buses is ignored. Nevertheless it is instructive to quantify it with figures representing realistic conditions. The initial values of the various parameters were taken as being:

$L = 3$ miles	$X_b = 3500$	$\beta = 5$ minutes
$S = 10$ m.p.h.		$\alpha = 10$ minutes
$i = 6.7$ m.p.h.	$X_c = 2380$	

All these figures, with the exception of ΔS, were estimated from traffic flow and bus occupancy data relating to radial roads into central Leicester at peak periods. An arbitrary value for ΔS of 1 m.p.h. was then chosen, and the value of ΔX_c calculated when $T_1 - T_2 = 0$. For $\Delta S = 1$ the value of ΔX_c for this 'breakeven' point was 641 and for $\Delta S = 5$ it was 3092. This means that according to the 'total journey time' criterion a movement of passengers from car to bus would be justified, so long as an increase of traffic flow speed of

1 m.p.h. could be achieved by a transfer of less than 641 passengers. If the ratio $\Delta S:\Delta X_c$ (for $\Delta S=1$) was greater than 1:641 a transfer of passengers to bus would increase the total journey times, since the gains of the original bus passengers and the 'continuing' car travellers would be more than offset by the losses of car-to-bus transferees.

Table 38 shows the 'breakeven' number of passengers who could be transferred from car to bus for a 1 m.p.h. increase in the average speed of the traffic flow, according to the total journey time criterion.

Table 38. Number of passengers per hour transferring from car to bus, with a 1 m.p.h. increase in average traffic speed, for a total journey time 'breakeven' position[1]

L=	3 miles	1 mile	0.5 miles
i =10 miles	527	296	178
9	554	306	184
5	743	373	214
4	829	401	226
2	1127	483	261
1	1410	548	286
0	1924	641	321

[1] $X_c=2380$; $\alpha=10$ mins; $\beta=5$ mins.
$X_b=3500$.

As would be expected, the position becomes worse (in the sense that a 1 m.p.h. increase in traffic flow speed must be achieved with a smaller transfer of passengers) as the average length of journey on the congested road becomes shorter and as the vehicle journey speed advantage of cars becomes greater. Thus when L=0.5 and i=10 m.p.h. it must be possible to achieve an increase in average traffic flow speed of 1 m.p.h. for the transfer of only 178 passengers in order to achieve the 'breakeven' position. For i=0 and L=3 miles the breakeven figure increases to 1,924 passengers. These low and high breakeven figures represent 7.5% and 80.8% respectively of all passengers originally travelling by car.

Table 39 shows the breakeven car transfer figure for any length of journey, when $\alpha=\beta$.

Table 39. Number of passengers per hour transferring from car to bus, with a 1 m.p.h. increase in traffic flow speed, for a total journey time 'breakeven' position, when bus and car terminal times are the same[1]

i m.p.h.	'Breakeven' transfer
10	866
9	931
5	1469
4	1780
2	3365
1	6578
0	∝

[1] $X_b = 3500$; $X_c = 2380$; $\alpha = \beta$.

The question now arises of how far the speed increases required to justify a car-to-bus transfer according to the total journey time criterion are attainable. The speed/flow relationship obtained by the Road Research Laboratory for central London roads in 1962* fits recent data for the relationship on roads in central Leicester fairly closely. This relationship (applying to speeds of 24 m.p.h. or less) is expressed in the linear equation

$$V = 28 - 0.00583Q$$

where V is the average speed of cars in the traffic flow and Q is the number of vehicles per hour (in passenger car units).†

If an average car load of 1.4 and an average peak bus load of 45 are assumed, and the adapted speed/flow equation

$$V = 28 - 0.00583 \left[\frac{3X_b}{45} + \frac{X_c}{1.4} \right]$$

is held to apply, then the transfer of 641 travellers from bus to car would increase average vehicle journey speeds by 2.4 m.p.h., so that the car-to-bus transfer would be justified on this criterion. If the average length of journey on the congested road, L, was only 0.5 miles the breakeven value of ΔX_c

* Smeed and Wardrop, *op cit.*, pp. 307–308.

† This formula was used for the first estimate of the value of i above (i = 6.7), given an average bus speed of 10 m.p.h. and a traffic flow of 1933 passenger car units.

would be 198.3 passengers, and if L=1 mile it would be 338.4 passengers. A car-to-bus transfer of 199 would give a speed increase of 0.8 m.p.h. and one of 339 passengers an increase of 1.3 m.p.h., so that the first transfer would bring a net increase in total door-to-door journey time, the second a small decrease.

The assumed speed/flow equation gives a speed increase of 1 m.p.h. ($\Delta S=1$) for every 265 passengers transferred from car to bus. This means that, of the possibilities examined in Table 38, the only cases where a car-to-bus transfer would not be justified (because the required speed increase could only be obtained by moving more than the breakeven number of passengers) are where L=0.5 miles and $i>4$ m.p.h. All the possible transfers in Table 39, where $\alpha=\beta$, would be justified.

The speed/flow formula used does not, of course, apply to all traffic conditions; generally for worse conditions the gain in speed (both as an absolute amount and as a percentage increase) from a given reduction in the traffic flow will be greater.*

The journey time formula used here assumes that both bus and car speeds will increase equally if the traffic flow is reduced (although different values have been given for the difference, i, between car and bus vehicle speeds, it is assumed that i remains constant after the car-to-bus transfer). But this assumption may not be justified for large speed increases, when the value of i may also increase. This means that continuing car travellers would gain more in reduced journey time than bus passengers, and the effect of a transfer on total journey times could be affected by the initial distribution of passengers between car and bus, savings of journey time being greater, *ceteris paribus*, the higher the original proportion of car travellers was to all travellers. The dropping of the assumption that the traffic flow is composed entirely of buses and of cars carrying commuters need not have a drastic effect on the calculations of journey time savings. Suppose that two new catagories of travellers, commercial vehicle (including lorry) drivers and through car travellers, were introduced. Then these would constitute a part of the traffic flow which

* Given a linear relationship $V=a-bQ$ the value of b will be greater for narrower roads or those with more intersections. Thus Wardrop's 1947 formula for all traffic on 30 ft. roads in central London was

$$V=25-0.014Q$$

The allowance for controlled intersections made by Smeed and Wardrop in the Central London study increases the value of b to approximately 0.0059 for the range of traffic flows to which a linear relationship is applicable.

could not be transferred to local buses, but they would benefit from increased traffic speeds in the same way as post-transfer car travellers. The inaccuracies resulting from including these classes of road users with car commuters, as has been done in the calculations made in this article, are that the car load figure of 1.4 is too high for both lorries and commercial vehicles, and that lorries are equivalent to more than one passenger car unit.

The practical implications of the use of the total journey time criterion for Leicester can only be very tentative, since its application involves detailed knowledge of the conditions on individual roads. The original bus and car passenger flow figures were, as mentioned above, based on estimates of flows on the city end of radial routes into Leicester, particularly London Road from the Evington Road junction to the junction with Granby Street and Charles Street. The speed flow formula also fits traffic data on the radial roads at peak periods approximately, though this is a matter on which more work is required than has been possible in this study. In order to obtain estimates of the actual running speeds of buses and cars at peak and non-peak periods, and of their respective terminal times, a number of runs were made from points outside central Leicester to places in the central area and *vice versa*. In each case the journey was made from a specific house or point in a suburban area to a specific destination in central Leicester by bus and car, both departing at the same time (but not always on the same day). For many

Table 40. Comparison of times for journeys to and from central Leicester, using car and bus

No. of trips[1]	Average total journey times, minutes		Average terminal times,[2] minutes		Average Vehicle journey speeds,[3] m.p.h.	
	Bus	Car	Bus	Car	Bus	Car
a. Peak periods						
15	26.20	19.30 (22.30)	13.00	9.40 (12.40)	11.00	15.68
b. Non-peak periods						
11	28.55	19.40 (22.40)	14.85	11.00 (14.00)	13.05	22.94

[1]Each pair of journeys by car and bus on identical routes is counted as one.
[2]This is taking an average time for putting the car into the car park (not including the time getting to the car park) of 3 minutes. This was based on a smaller sample than the other figures. For multi-storey car parks parking time was about 6 minutes, so that alternative total and terminal times are shown in brackets.
[3]These were the speeds on the part of the total journey covered by the bus route. Car running off the bus route was included under terminal times.

of the peak hour journeys the same trip was made twice; on an inwards direction in the morning peak period and outwards during the evening peak. Most of the trips made are shown in Figure 4, and the main results of the survey are shown in Table 40.

The range of differences in total terminal time (α—β) was therefore from 3.60 to 3.85 minutes. Six peak and three non-peak pairs of journeys were made in which the obvious car route was different from the bus route. The average car speed for the whole journey for peak periods was 14.56 m.p.h. and for non-peak periods 19.04 m.p.h. The corresponding bus vehicle speeds were 9.82 m.p.h. and 14.2 m.p.h. An approximately linear relationship existed between the observed car and bus speeds over the range of car speeds of 6–24 m.p.h. With car speeds as S_1 and bus speeds as S_2 the relationship was

$$S_2 = 3.12 + 0.48S_1$$

which expressed in terms of i gives

$$i = -3.12 + 0.52S_1$$

It is dangerous to make any very definite statements about whether a car-to-bus transfer would be justified according to the total journey time criterion. The data collected in this study is not really good enough for this. In particular better estimates of i and α and β are required and the speed-flow relationship needs to be tested for different roads. The speed-flow figures available for Leicester are averages for lengths of road including congested inner stretches and outer parts with much higher running speeds. The estimated bus and car passenger mix also varies for different parts of the main radial routes into the city. In so far as any generalizations can be made about Leicester it would appear that conditions are approaching the critical position when a car-to-bus transfer would be justified. The value of i even at the lowest estimate was fairly high, and the disadvantage of buses in relation to terminal times was about the same as that assumed in the model. Unless the average length of journey on any congested road was three miles or more which is improbable it therefore seems unlikely at the moment that traffic would be speeded up sufficiently by a 'compulsory' car-to-bus transfer to justify this. If we take as estimates of the figures for routes into central Leicester the values obtained in the survey for peak and non-peak periods (combined peak and non-peak $L=2.72$; peak $S=11.0$, $i=4.68$, $\alpha=13.0$, $\beta=9.4$; Non-peak $S=13.05$, $i=9.89$, $\alpha=14.85$, $\beta=11.0$) then the breakeven

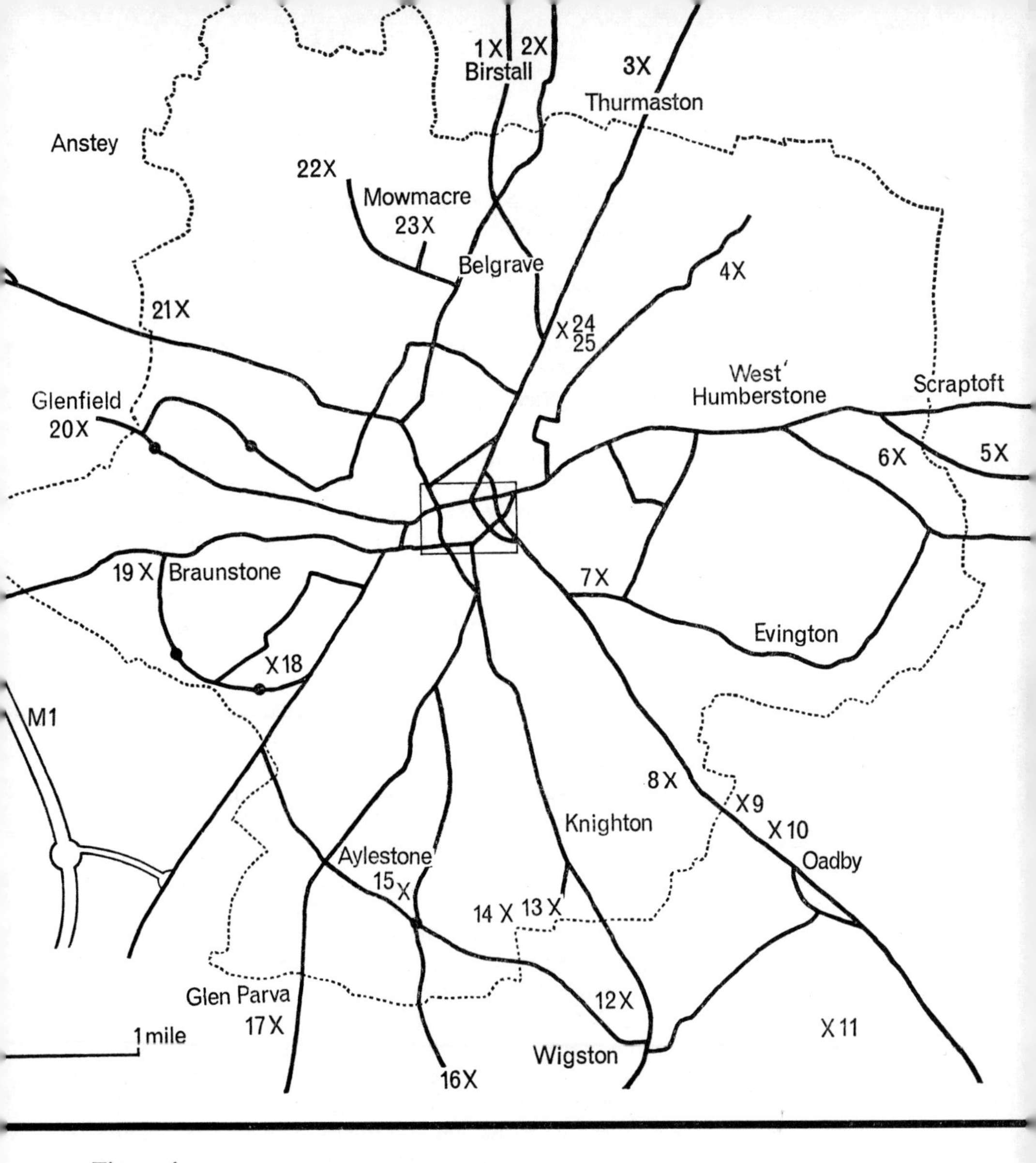

Figure 4.
Leicester traffic survey: map showing routes taken and reference number for each trip

transfers for a 1 m.p.h. increase would be 780.2 and 439.9 passengers respectively. But the sample is too small and the variability of the data too great for any conclusions to be drawn. There are almost certainly short periods at peak times on some days when a transfer would result in shorter average journey times, but it is difficult to see how constraints could be applied only for a period of ten to twenty minutes. On the other hand it seems very likely that any further transfer of passengers from bus to car will cause average journey times to lengthen, and that a policy seeking to discourage such a transfer would be justified – if the shorter journey time criterion is accepted, that is. The Smeed and Wardrop study showed that a transfer of all car travellers to buses in central London conditions would increase average (and therefore total) journey times for journeys of one mile or less and with parking times of less than eight minutes. For three-mile journeys average journey times would decrease by 4% if parking times was zero and by 11% if it was ten minutes.*

If the various problems of measurement discussed here could be overcome, would the criterion of reduced total door-to-door journey time be an acceptable policy guide? Perhaps the main theoretical difficulty is that there is no weighting of time savings, those of all travellers being valued equally. Some people value time savings more than others, and if one of the three classes of travellers (original bus passengers, continuing car travellers and car-to-bus transferees) put a larger or smaller average value per minute on its time savings than the others the calculations of net benefit would be affected. It could be argued that those willing to pay more to travel to work more quickly by car value their time savings more than those using buses. If a tax were to force some car users into buses, it would follow that those still using cars would be those willing to pay more for the speed advantage. As has been argued elsewhere in discussing the case for a general congestion tax, however, willingness to pay will mainly reflect income levels, and it depends on our value judgment whether this is taken to be an adequate measure of the value of time savings to the community. Weighting time savings by some willingness-to-pay or consumers'-suplus type criterion would probably give the greatest weight to continuing car travellers, the next largest weight to car-to-bus transferees, and the smallest to original bus passengers. The net effect of such weighting is impossible to estimate except with specific figures, as the losses (increased door-to-door journey times) of the car-to-bus transferees, and the

* Smeed and Wardrop, *op. cit.*, p. 110.

gains of the continuing car travellers, would both be made more important. The use of a form of congestion tax or of increased parking charges as a means of bringing about the transfer would be more efficient than an undiscriminating ban on private cars, because it would allow some choice between bus and car travel according to individual evaluations of time savings.

In making estimates of the gains from a car-to-bus transfer, however, it would not seem to be worthwhile to try to put different values on the time savings of different people when almost all of them will be making work journeys. A system of weighting (apart, that is, from the 'automatic' weighting according to income which would result from the unquestioning use of the price mechanism envisaged by some advocates of a congestion tax) would be complicated, could only be based on very imperfect information, and would not yield any great advantage.

There is another main problem in using the reduction of total door-to-door journey times as a criterion for the justification of mandatory action designed to bring about a car-to-bus transfer. This arises when the dynamic rather than the static situation is considered. If present trends continue the value of the parameters of the measuring equations will change constantly and, as has already been argued, they will tend to make the time savings from a transfer greater. The policy issue therefore arises of how far ahead of the trends mandatory action to secure a car-to-bus transfer would be justified. To wait until conditions had deteriorated to the point at which a transfer would be justified on the reduced-journey-time criterion could be to wait too long. By this time public transport might be so run down that it would not be quickly or easily expanded again to take the transferred traffic. On the other hand, to act too soon would obviously be unjustified. This problem is closely related to the important issue, which is largely outside the scope of the present discussion, of the means by which the transfer would be secured. It is obviously more difficult to discriminate between different roads if parking restrictions are the chosen method of control than if a form of congestion tax is used. If parking restrictions were the main method of bringing about a transfer, then the effective choice of where to induce a car-to-bus transfer, and where not to, might lie between different urban centres rather than between individual roads. Nevertheless the journey time criterion could be used and the results for different routes aggregated. A complication connected with parking restrictions is that a change in these would itself affect the relationship between a car-to-bus transfer and total journey times.

A transfer of travellers from car to bus is one of the few measures which would lead rapidly to a significant improvement in the level of congestion on urban roads. A measurement of the effect on total journey time seems to be the most straightforward criterion for distinguishing between those road conditions on which 'compulsory' methods of transfer should be applied, and those where they are not yet appropriate. A tentative conclusion of this study is that it would be difficult to justify a policy aimed at forcing people back on to buses at present in Leicester, but much easier to show that any further transfer from bus to car should be discouraged.

6

Methods of bringing about a car-to-bus passenger transfer

If one aim of transport policy should be to reverse or check the drift from public to private transport in large urban areas then the question of how such a policy should be carried out must be considered. As has already been argued it is very unlikely that improvements in bus services alone will be effective in halting the transfer from bus to car. In the actual choice situation faced by individuals the car is likely to continue to offer a superior service to the bus because as the roads become more congested, and car journeys take longer, so must the service offered by buses deteriorate as well. It is only by the collective decision of a number of people that a transfer from car to bus could bring about a large enough improvement in journey speeds to offset the longer terminal times normally associated with bus travel. Except when parking conditions are very difficult or terminal travelling times insignificant, the individual will almost always be better off, in terms of travelling time, by using a car than by using a bus because the car advantage in terminal time will not be offset by the very small increase in journey time on the congested road caused by removing only one car from it. The advantage of the shorter average journey time criterion discussed in the last chapter is that it provides a means of deciding when a collective decision to transfer from car to bus (or not to transfer from bus to car) would benefit the community as a whole. The purpose of this chapter is, then, to discuss possible measures for bringing about desirable changes in the mode of travel by influencing collective decisions.

One obvious way of attempting to win back passengers for the buses would be to reverse the trend of recent years and lower bus fares. There are several ways in which a reduction of bus fares might be made possible. If those undertakings like the Midland Red which provide many rural services were relieved of the financial burden of these then some lowering of fares would become possible. But the services of undertakings operating almost entirely inside urban areas, as do most municipal undertakings, would clearly not benefit from the subsidization of rural services. Where the present boundary system leads to a wasteful use of resources some fare reductions could follow abolition of the system, but the gains would probably be only marginal. Differential peak and non-peak pricing could have some effect on demand, though, as shown in Chapter 3, it is not always clear whether peak services should be priced higher or lower than those in non-peak periods. It might be that the whole cost of peak operation is marginal in the sense that the buses and crews would not be needed at all if they were not to run, and that even some garage space and central overheads could also be saved. The cost of operation is also increased in peak periods by slower running and higher consequent labour costs per vehicle mile. Whether or not the whole of the extra costs is offset by the better load factor in peak periods is uncertain. If the operation of an off-peak bus had a marginal cost of 25*d.* per vehicle mile (fuel and wage costs), if average total costs were 43*d.* per vehicle mile, and if peak and off-peak mileages were equal this would suggest that the maximum cost which could be attributed to peak running would be 61*d.* per vehicle mile. If the average peak load was 45 passengers per mile, then the peak costs could be 1.35*d.* per vehicle mile and the off-peak costs (with an assumed load of 10 passengers per vehicle mile) would be 2.5*d.* per vehicle mile. But if off-peak marginal costs included only fuel and other running costs marginal cost pricing would suggest a lower off-peak price unless the load factor was less than about 5 persons per vehicle mile.

Really large cuts in bus fares could probably only be made if bus undertakings received a subsidy from the state or from local authorities. It seems doubtful whether such a subsidy would be justified. It could easily lead to greater pressure for wage increases and a general inflation of costs. There is no adequate information available about the cross elasticities of demand between bus and car travel, but it may well be that even if buses were free there would not be a significant movement from cars to buses at peak travel periods. If free buses became more crowded with former pedestrians the quality of service could deteriorate so that motorists became even less likely to transfer to buses. Although any possible measure to reduce bus fares, short of the payment of a subsidy, is obviously highly desirable it seems very doubtful whether such a reduction, even coupled with an improved service, would bring about a large enough swing back to public transport to make a significant reduction in the level of congestion.

If reducing the cost of bus services is not likely by itself to bring about the desired transfer from car to bus the possibility of raising the cost of motoring must also be considered. This could be achieved by imposing a congestion tax on cars using urban roads by increasing the rate of existing taxes on motorists, or by raising the cost of parking.

The proposal to put a congestion tax on all vehicles using certain roads was examined in the Ministry of Transport report *Road Pricing*,* and, with slightly less enthusiasm, in the subsequent report *Better Use of Town Roads*.† It has proved attractive to economists as a single measure which could theoretically bring about an optimum use of road space, not only between cars and buses but between different car users, and indeed between all forms of road traffic. Some of the wider claims made for the advantages of a congestion tax can be criticized.‡ The tax would allocate road space solely according to ability to pay and this might have socially undesirable consequences. It could result in a transfer of passengers from car to bus which would be rejected by the 'shorter journey time' criterion because average journey times would be lengthened. This would be because the time savings of those continuing to use their cars would be weighted more heavily than the possible time losses of car-to-bus transferees although the 'need' for the latter for faster travel might be less only in so far as they belonged to a lower income group than those still travelling by car. The congestion tax also suffers from the disadvantage that it cannot be easily or quickly introduced. It would require the use of fairly elaborate electronic equipment, and there would be considerable political difficulties connected with its introduction. Any lengthy delays could be very costly if, in the meanwhile, congestion worsened and the services offered by bus undertakings deteriorated rapidly. On the other hand a congestion tax would have considerable advantages as a means of bringing about a bus to car transfer where it was already clear that such a transfer would be desirable. Subject to the reservation about unequal income distribution, it would give some freedom of choice to consumers and enable those with a greater need for car travel, such as people living a long way from a bus stop, or suffering from some physical disability, to pay for the right to continue to use their cars.

The problem of changing the existing tax structure is complicated in that the two elements in the taxation of road vehicles, that of a straightforward

* *Road Pricing: The Economic and Technical Possibilities*, Ministry of Transport, 1964.
† *Better Use of Town Roads*, Ministry of Transport, 1967.
‡ C. H. Sharp. 'Congestion and Welfare,' *Economic Journal*, December 1966.

revenue raising tax, and that of charging a price for road track, have never been clearly distinguished. There is a strong case for reducing or abolishing the tax on fuel used by buses in order to help them to survive financially in what must be a very difficult immediate future (unless measures to increase the use of buses are suddenly and dramatically successful). But as a measure to bring about a car-to-bus transfer it is doubtful whether this would be very effective. As already argued it seems likely that the demand for bus transport is inelastic over existing price ranges, and that a reduction in present fares is unlikely to bring about much increase in their use. The other alternative is to increase taxation on cars. Now the taxes falling on car users, purchase tax, licence duty and fuel tax could clearly be raised to levels which would limit car ownership or reduce car use. Fuel tax in particular could be used to bring about an immediate decrease in motoring. But the obvious disadvantage of such action is that it would fall on all motorists and would not discriminate against the use of congested urban roads. The charge levied through taxation on the users of uncongested rural roads is already probably considerably higher than the cost of providing and maintaining these roads. A congestion tax would be a much more suitable means of bringing about a car-to-bus transfer than an increase in fuel tax.

If all parking spaces in the central City area were controlled by the Corporation or some other public body, then it would be possible to restrict all commuter and other traffic requiring parking space in this area. There would, of course, be no control over through traffic, and the unloading and loading of commercial vehicles would present a distinct problem. But control of the peak commuter and other stopping traffic should be sufficient to deal with the present problem of congestion in Leicester. There are three main ways in which parking restrictions could be imposed. These are by outright bans, by the variation of permitted waiting times, and by a system of charges. Before exploring these possibilities the present parking situation in Leicester may be surveyed.

There are four forms of car parking in central Leicester, controlled on-street parking, public off-street car parks, private off-street parking, and multi-storey car parks. In the central area there are no meters, but 30-minute, 60-minute and 2-hour limits on on-street parks during the working day. The approximate capacity of roads permitting 30-minute, 60-minute and 2-hour parking was 211–231 vehicles, 1255–1370 venicles, and 135–148 vehicles respectively on a recent count. This makes a total of 1601–1749 vehicles (depending upon average vehicle length.) This central parking area stretched approximately from the Burleys Way–Belgrave roundabout in the north to London Road Station and Welford Road junction in the south, and from the Humberstone Road–Brunswick Street junction in the east to West Bridge Street and Western Boulevard in the west. It was therefore only a strictly limited City centre area. There were, in a survey made in September 1966, ten public off-street car parks. The total capacity of these was 1598 vehicles. The only estimate available of the capacity of private off-street car parks is that contained in the Leicester Traffic Plan. This showed a total capacity of 3400 cars within approximately the same central area as that described for on-street parking. The total capacity of the three multi-storey car parks according to the City Engineer's 'Motorists' Guide' of July 1966 was 2030 cars. The total parking capacity of the central area according to these estimates was 8283–8398 vehicles.

The survey made by the City Engineer's Department, in which Mr Usher also took part, on 6 September 1966, provided arrival and departure figures for the off-street public car parks for quarter hour periods throughout the day. This has been analysed to show how many of the cars arriving before 9.0 A.M. did not leave the park until after 12.30 P.M. This figure should be a reasonably good estimate of the volume of commuter traffic using the parks.

The results of this estimation are shown in Table 41. Figures were also obtained for Lee Circle and Hamshaw's multi-storey parks and these showed

Table 41. Estimates of use by commuters of off-street public car parks, Leicester central parking area, 6 September 1966

Car park	Capacity	Estimated number of commuter cars	% of park capacity filled by 9.0 A.M.
Dunkirk Street	168	66	56.5
St. Peter's Lane	350	123	45.7
Dover Street	75	63	100.0
Ashwell Street	75	43	64.0
Burley's Way	150	56	48.0
Midland Street	110	57	61.8
Welford Road	150	80	67.3
St. Matthew's	100	34	41.0
The Newarke	120	101	91.7
Wellington Street	300	159	60.7
TOTALS	1598	782	59.6

that there was very little 'casual' commuter traffic but that there were 180 reserved places in Lee Circle and 111 in Hamshaw's which were presumably used by regular commuters. The figures in Table 41 suggest that there is still parking space for some expansion of commuter car traffic and that the total proportion using public off-street car parks was relatively small. On the basis of the Leicester Traffic Plan estimate of approximately 8,100 cars entering Inner Leicester (approximately the same area as the central traffic area) on the sample day in 1963 it would seem that only about 9–10% were using public off-street parks. In order to be able to influence traffic flows through parking it would be necessary to control much more of central area parking than at present. Since the multi-storey parks do not cater for large numbers of commuter cars the great majority must use private off-street parks, and the figure of 3,400 may be an underestimate. There are also many uncontrolled streets outside the central area where commuter cars may park and travellers still walk into the centre. The traffic flow figures at present available do not show clearly how much congestion is caused by traffic moving to places outside the central area (some of which will cross through the centre). In Birmingham it is estimated that only 30% of bus passengers travel to the city centre area.* Use of parking restrictions as a method of traffic control would involve obtaining powers to control private parking (beyond the long-term control through Town Planning legislation), and extending the regulation of on-street parking to a much wider area of Leicester than at present. If a sufficiently wide public control of parking was achieved to make this a powerful means of restricting commuter traffic the question would arise of who should exercise the control. There is at present no wholly suitable authority. Neither the police nor local authorities are necessarily equipped to carry out policies attempting to bring about an optimum car/bus modal split to reconcile the sometimes opposing interests of shopowners, industrialists, motorists and bus passengers. Unless very clear guiding lines were established centrally it is probable that either a new *ad hoc* authority would have to be set up or decisions would need to be made by the Ministry of Transport after local enquiries. If these difficulties were overcome, and there was an authority with an adequate control of parking in Leicester, and it was decided to place some restraint on commuter car traffic then there would be various possible ways of achieving this objective. All day or four-hour parking (Leicester is still small enough to make a return to homes in the lunchtime possible for

* Information given by Mr J. Isaac, Deputy Traffic Manager, Birmingham and Midland Motor Omnibus Co.

many workers) could be limited to the maximum number of cars required. But this presupposes that the optimum number of cars could be calculated and would allow no choice to consumers at all. It would also mean that traffic would be admitted on a first come, first served principle and people living nearest to the city centre would find it easier to get parking space than those further away whose need might be presumed to be greater. There would also be uncertainty about whether parking space was available, and commuters might be forced to arrive unnecessarily early in order to secure themselves a place. This is what may happen anyhow, under the present system, if commuter traffic grows and as is likely, car parking space cannot be greatly expanded. This limitation of parking space, incidentally, raises some doubts about some tong-term predictions of the future levels of commuter traffic. The Leicester Traffic Plan, for example, forecasts a possible morning peak flow of 36,700 vehicles into Inner Leicester by 1995, but it is clearly possible that lack of parking space may prevent such a level of demand from developing in reality. The alternative to a rigid 'quota system' for car parking space would to be to use the price mechanism, and make parking space available at very much higher rates than at present. Current charges in off-street public parks in Leicester are only 1*s.* 3*d.* for four hours and 2*s.* 6*d.* for the whole day. Restriction of parking space through price (with heavy discrimination against the commuter wishing to use the park for four hours or more) would have the advantage of allowing those whose need was more urgent to buy parking space, and there would be less uncertainty since people could buy season tickets. But it has the same disadvantage as the congestion tax that the 'need' measured mainly reflects wealth, and it would not necessarily be those living away from suitable public transport, or those who were not fit to walk to bus stops, who would be able to buy parking space. Possibly a pricing system with some machinery for granting cheap parking tickets to hardship cases would be the best solution, though this is open to the usual objections about the 'growth of bureaucracy,' and would certainly use up considerable manpower if it was applied all over the country.

With the existing very limited degree of public control of parking in Leicester about the only policy likely to have much effect on persuading motorists to travel by bus (or travel outside the peak periods) would be to attempt to discourage shoppers travelling in the peak periods by car by persuading them to travel by bus, or, as is more likely, to travel outside the peak period. This could be done by prohibiting all on-street parking in the central area between 8.30 and 9.30 A.M., though the numbers of shoppers and other short-term car parkers travelling at this time is probably not large enough to make the gains more than marginal.

As well as reducing the price of bus travel or increasing the cost of motoring, a car-to-bus passenger transfer could be encouraged by legal restrictions on the use of urban roads by private cars. A general ban on cars in city centres, which is proposed, for example, in the Leicester Traffic Plan, raises issues which go beyond the scope of this study as this would only be possible after considerable investment in car parks and the completion of major new road schemes. But one proposal which commends itself to bus undertakings, and which would not involve major investment, is that one lane of roads used by buses should be preserved for buses alone. This raises some difficult problems for both road engineers and economists. It presupposes that at least a four lane highway is available (unless buses had one exclusive lane which carried inwards traffic in the morning and outwards traffic at night while the reverse flow used non-reserved lanes) and since the bus would need an inside lane in order to pick up and put down passengers, other traffic would have to cross the bus lane at all intersections and to obtain access to premises at the road side. This might not be a great problem however as the bus lane would be relatively lightly used in terms of vehicle flow (though it would need to carry a heavy passenger flow to be justified). The main difficulty would, of course, be the extra congestion caused to cars and commercial vehicles. The proposal seems to have enough to recommend it to justify a study of the types of road on which it would be most appropriate, and the costs and benefits likely to result. One problem here would be the need to work with estimated traffic flows since the project would not be likely to be justified unless it was assumed that a considerable volume of passenger traffic would transfer from cars back to buses (and perhaps some additional traffic be generated).

7

The railways

Perhaps the most important fact about the railways as a means of urban transportation is that they are there. Building new roads or widening those that are already there involves large-scale new investment and taking away scarce urban land from some alternative use. Forms of transport like the monorail or the underground railway which may not use up surface land will nevertheless necessitate heavy capital expenditure. Some rail lines, on the other hand, have surplus capacity available for extra passenger trains which can be run with very little capital expenditure and no extra demand for land at all. Some rail routes may even have a significant number of empty seats on existing commuter trains. But perhaps the greatest advantage of the railways is that they are not affected by congestion and can provide a

Table 42. Passenger flows between Leicester stations and major destinations, 1965

Destination	Outwards tickets sold	Inwards tickets sold	Total
London	366,278	n.a.	—
Nottingham	132,114	128,306	260,420
Birmingham	81,728	n.a.	—
Loughborough	63,952	111,243	175,195
Kettering	48,023	67,496	105,519
Derby	36,255	54,675	90,930
Syston	31,589	40,384	71,973
Manchester	26,169	n.a.	—
Market Harborough	26,087	119,070	145,157
Hinckley	23,567	76,983	100,550
Sileby	15,017	76,713	91,730
Melton Mowbray	12,466	61,392	73,858
Barrow on Soar	12,369	43,472	55,841
Narborough	11,796	52,025	63,821
Rugby	11,389	n.a.	—
Sheffield	11,238	n.a.	—
Leeds	10,063	n.a.	—

high speed service so that journeys of any length by rail may be considerably quicker than by car. The obvious question therefore arises of why urban rail lines are not everywhere used to their full capacity.

In Leicester estimates suggest that rail did not carry more than 0.7–0.8% of total passenger traffic in 1965–66.

The passenger flow between Leicester stations (London Road, Central and Humberstone Road) and major destinations (measured as having total annual sales of tickets from Leicester stations of more than 10,000 in 1965) are shown in Table 42.

These figures do not represent the true balance of inwards and outwards passenger traffic as return tickets from each station were recorded as two outward journeys from that station. Thus stations with regular commuter traffic into Leicester would be expected to show an apparently unbalanced inwards flow. These figures illustrate the great importance of the long distance flow of passengers to London, and suggest that the main flows of commuter and shopping traffic to Leicester were from Loughborough, Market Harborough, Kettering, Hinckley, Sileby, Melton Mowbray, Syston, Narborough and Barrow on Soar. Of these places Barrow, Sileby, Syston and Narborough are within the 'Greater Leicester' area (see Figure 1).

There are at least three immediate reasons why the railways play such a small part in carrying commuter traffic in Leicester. The main lines open today are not particularly well placed for passenger traffic and some of the stations are not very convenient for the main residential areas. Thus southeast Leicester and the developing residential areas of Oadby and Wigston have never had any rail line serving them. Stations which might have carried commuter traffic like Belgrave and Birstall and Rothley have been closed and the lines running through both the eastern and western suburbs have been closed. A crucial factor affecting the demand for rail transport in Leicester is probably the relative nearness of the outer residential suburbs to the centre. Many commuter journeys would not be long enough for the greater speed of the rail journey to affect the terminal times involved in getting to and from the stations, when the total rail journey time is compared with total car journey time. The amount of severely congested road on the average day may also not be enough to make the car 'main haul' journey very much slower than the rail main haul.

Allowing for the disadvantages of the railways for carrying commuter traffic in Leicester however it seems reasonable to argue that general rail policy has also been partly responsible for the very small proportion of passenger traffic carried. The attempt by British Rail to follow the goal of profitability, both under Dr Beeching and subsequently, has led to an attitude towards commuter traffic which is highly debatable if any wider objective than immediate profitability for the railways is considered. In their calculations about the profitability of different lines the railways have usually considered whole routes, such as the former line from Leicester Belgrave Gate to Marefield Junction and Melton Mowbray, and have not considered the possibility of keeping open short commuter routes only. They have also based their calculations of losses on the existing situation, making no allowance for the possible growth of commuter traffic. At least until very recently railway closure policy has been considered in isolation from the rest of transport policy. The possible impact on the demand for commuter travel by rail of growing congestion and of possible measures to restrict the free use of private cars on urban roads has been disregarded. The procedure for appealing against a decision to close a branch line can almost be described as farcical. The Transport Users Consultative Committees have only been able to consider arguments about hardship which would follow from a rail closure, and the proceedings have largely been taken up with descriptions of endless similar cases of people who were made sick by bus travel or mothers who could find no room for a pram on the local bus service. There has been no established technique for evaluating these hardships, and all the more important economic arguments about the effect of a rail closure have been considered to be outside the matters which the T.U.C.C. could consider. A case based on economic arguments can be made direct to the Minister, but, since these arguments are more important than those about individual cases of hardship, the procedure at the public hearings would seem to be largely a waste of time. But the main way in which the existing system of making railway closures may give a wrong answer is, of course, that some of the most important costs and benefits are ignored if the immediate profitability of the rail line is the only consideration. When a station or a branch line that has been carrying some commuter traffic is closed some people will be diverted to private transport. The extra cars which will run on what are likely to be already congested roads may very well entail slower journeys for those who used to travel by train compared with their former train journey. But even more important, the existing traffic flow will be slowed down by the additional cars and a very large number of people may have to put up with slower work journeys. The value to the community of the lost time of these road users may be greater than the losses formerly being made by the closed rail line. In 1965 the railways proposed to close all passenger stations on the Bromsgrove to Birmingham and Redditch to Birmingham lines (which join at Barnt Green). This would undoubtedly have added significantly to the already severe congestion existing on the Bristol and Pershore roads. Whether the benefits accruing to road travellers in not having the rail commuter traffic adding to the congestion on these roads was equivalent to the losses on these rail lines is debatable, but the calculations, with some allowance for predictable future changes, ought to be made. In this particular instance permission to close the rail stations was refused by the Minister, but rail services have since been cut very considerably.

At the present time it seems unlikely that any more commuter lines will be closed, and Leicester was perhaps unlucky in losing so many commuter stations before their potential value was realized. But current rail policy in regard to commuter traffic is still far from satisfactory. Rail pricing policy which is still guided by the need to seek to make a profit (or minimize losses) and ignore all other considerations does nothing to encourage commuter traffic and may well discourage it. In some areas such as Birmingham cheap day return tickets are no longer available from many of the nearer suburban stations (and in some cases longer journeys may be cheaper than shorter ones) and commuters have been faced with a sharp increase in price. Sometime before the threatened closure of the Bromsgrove to New Street passenger stations, for example, the cheap day tickets from the suburb of Northfield and all stations from there into Birmingham were abolished. Outside London the railways seem to make little attempt to encourage commuter traffic by advertising or providing large car parks round suburban stations. Now this may make sense given the profitability objective imposed on the railways since highly peaked commuter traffic is rarely profitable, but it does not necessarily make such good sense in the context of a national transport policy.

In Leicester there is a *prima facie* case for making a study of the possibility of the railways making a more significant contribution to the carriage of passenger traffic. The first requirement of a detailed study would be to estimate the surplus capacity already existing in peak periods on the lines running into Leicester. This would be made up of regular empty seats on existing services, plus the extra coaches which could be added to existing trains, plus new stopping trains which could be fitted into the timetable. The capacity of the existing stations would limit the possibility of adding new passenger trains to the timetable. The technical and economic implications of re-opening closed passenger lines, of the operation of new short-distance commuter services, and of the opening of new stations on existing lines could then be considered. In all the calculations it would be necessary to consider future as well as existing traffic flows. The kind of new services which might be developed may be described briefly, and also tentatively, since no work has been done on technical or economic feasibility. The existing main line through London Road station might in future support a short-distance commuter service stopping at Syston, Thurmaston (new station), Gipsy Lane area (new station), Humberstone Road, London Road, Wigston Fields (new station) and South Wigston (former station, track now removed). The Central station line might have a similar service from Birstall through to Aylestone, Whetstone and Cosby. To re-open the old line from the former Belgrave Road station would no doubt require major new investment, but it should not be ruled out in any study of possible rail development since the former track serves a continuous area of development as far as Bushby, though Belgrave Road station itself is inconveniently located for central Leicester. These possible rail developments ought to be examined before heavy investment was sanctioned in any new development such as an urban motorway or a monorail system.

8

Conclusions

The basic dilemma of urban passenger transport in Britain today is that people are increasingly choosing the superior service which can be supplied by private car ownership, while the community is unwilling, or unable, to provide the road space required for unlimited car access to city centres. Studies which have attempted long-term projections of demand for car transport like *Traffic in Towns* and the Leicester Traffic Plan have shown that even if the cost of providing for the potential demand for travelling by car in city centre areas could be met, the provision of the necessary road space would destroy the town as a place to live and in which to work and shop. American experience has already, to some extent, borne out this conclusion.

Some of the gloomier pictures which have been painted of the future everlasting traffic jams and road chaos may be exaggerated, since, if new roads and additional parking space are not provided the projected growth in car travel may not take place. Parking is a particularly important constraint, since, however congested the roads become, cars will still provide a quicker door-to-door journey so long as car terminal travelling times are shorter. But even if all the forecasts of conditions at the end of the century cannot be wholly accepted, it is clear that an intolerable level of congestion is being reached in more and more cities. The present modal split between public and private transport can be judged to be inefficient by a criterion which should have the merit of being widely acceptable, if it can be shown that average door-to-door journey times would be shorter if more people travelled by bus or train, and fewer by private car.

A detailed examination of the cost and revenue structure of the two bus undertakings operating in Leicester showed that urban services were still at present able to be financially self-supporting, but that their position was deteriorating. The concept of what is an unremunerative service has not always been clearly defined in the past, but if this is equated as nearly as possible with covering the relevant marginal cost, then there were not many bus trips in Leicester which were unremunerative, except for those running on Sundays. Services running out into the country were, as might be expected, often earning insufficient revenue to cover the appropriate level of marginal cost. The examination of bus costs showed the great importance of peak traffic in pushing up cost levels, and suggested that a really determined effort to stagger demand could provide a most important means of improving bus services and reducing the level of congestion. It is not considered that there is at present any case for a general subsidy to support urban bus services. It is unlikely that a reduction in fares would, by itself, bring back many passengers to the buses, and there is no clear evidence to show that recent increases have had any effect on the rate of deline of bus use. The financial position of bus undertakings is, however, likely to deteriorate, and consideration should be given to reducing or moving the burden of fuel tax. It is also possible that some undertakings may find new investment difficult in the future, and some government assistance may be required if they are to hold or win back passenger traffic.

There is a strong case for arguing that the present system whereby bus undertakings are supposed to cross-subsidize their rural routes from earnings on their high-density urban routes should be abolished. The whole subject of rural transport needs an up-to-date investigation leading to a decision on how far it is still considered desirable today to provide below-cost transport for those living in the country, and, where it is desirable, who should pay for it. There are various costs and benefits which might result from a decision to restrict rural bus transport to that which could be provided without subsidization. There would be a cost to the community if housing and services existing in rural areas were not fully used, and if there was a movement of population from the country into the towns which involved extra house building and the provision of services, and increased traffic congestion. There would be a loss, which it would be very difficult to quantify, to those who continued to live in the country and who could no longer travel into a town to enjoy the amenities provided there. There would be some increase in urban congestion from a greater use of cars by people travelling in from the country, though as this would tend to be outside the peak journey-to-work time it would be unlikely to be serious. It seems unlikely that there is a large group of people living in the country and working in the town who could not afford to pay the full cost of some form of public transport to get them to work. Agriculture might suffer if rural transport deteriorated in that it might prove more difficult to get workers, or to keep them. The needs of the rural areas should be evaluated in the light of present conditions when motor cars, television, and such developments as mobile shops and libraries have all had an impact on the nature of life in the country. In so far as a need still exists for some kind of public provision of transport services, the best ways of meeting this need should be examined. Any subsidies required need not all be met from the same source. If it is national policy to prevent a drift of population into the urban areas from the country, then any necessary transport subsidy should come from the state, either directly, or through local authorities. If agricultural workers cannot afford essential travel into the towns then there might be a better case for examining their wage structure and farm prices than for subsidizing rural buses. If there is a national duty to make it possible for old age pensioners living in the country to visit the towns, then it might be more efficient to increase their pensions by a bonus similar to that paid to many workers because of the extra cost of living in London, and to operate bus services charging fares high enough to be self-supporting. There seems to be no good reason at all for expecting urban users of public transport to subsidize rural bus services. Such a subsidy cannot be supported by any value judgment and has the harmful effect of increasing the demand for private motoring on urban roads. It has also been a reason for the persistence of the 'boundary system' with its undesirable effects on bus operation.

The survey showed that in Leicester provision of bus services to the central urban areas by one undertaking, and to the other suburban areas by another, resulted in a wasteful use of resources and unnecessary complications in route planning. An equally good service could have been provided by a single undertaking with fewer bus trips and a higher load factor. On the Oadby route it seems likely that a more frequent through service could attract more passengers. There is a theoretical case for suggesting that in some outer districts a more frequent single central route would make a better use of fixed resources than three separate routes serving different parts of the same suburban area. Although more of the disadvantages of the present system could be overcome by instituting joint and coordinated services this would involve lengthy negotiation, would be wasteful of executive manpower, and still tend to inflexibility in an industry in which the pattern of demand can change quite rapidly. Since the main reason for the present boundary system would be removed if the need for cross-subsidization were removed then it is concluded that all the bus services in the Greater Leicester area should be provided by one undertaking. This raises the problem of the rural services at present operated by the Midland Red organization jointly with their urban Leicester services. The best solution would probably be to create a new undertaking operating services in the present Leicester Division of Midland Red and in the Leicester City area, though this is a matter on which final judgment could not be passed without further study. Whether it is necessary to continue to run all the rural services now operating would be determined after the review of rural transport already suggested. Quite apart from the issue of the rural services it would be short-sighted to confine a single Greater Leicester transport undertaking to the present built-up urban area. The development of new urban centres envisaged in The East Midlands Study, for example, will involve important new demand for urban-type passenger transport partly in the existing Midland Red Leicester Division. There are those who believe that bus undertakings become increasingly inefficient beyond a certain size. This is a matter of opinion which has not been conclusively demonstrated, but even if there are significant diseconomies of scale it is unlikely that the size of the proposed undertaking, which would have about 560 buses, would be too great. The exact boundaries of the new undertaking would need to be determined after some further investigation and there would be particular problems in the Coventry area.

What is true for Leicester would appear to be true, with some modifications, for the rest of the country. Obviously there would be considerable problems in drawing the boundary between different transport undertakings, and this could be much more difficult in the larger conurbations than in Leicester. But it is very difficult to see what can be gained from having two or more major bus undertakings responsible for the services in any one area. There is no real competition since the routes of each undertaking are protected, and the planning or variation of routes serving one area must be more difficult if it is the responsibility of several undertakings some of which may have conflicting interests. The traffic areas of these single undertakings would, of course, be based on existing and potential traffic flows and in most cases it should not be too difficult to find a boundary which constituted a 'watershed' between two sets of traffic flows. There does not seem to be any particularly strong reason for setting up purely urban or 'conurbation' transport authorities. Certainly in Leicester the buses serving the surrounding countryside could be advantageously coordinated with the urban buses in a single undertaking. This does not mean that the main bus undertaking in each area should necessarily have a complete monopoly of all services. There is no reason why some small undertakings should not be allowed to run in the villages wherever the major undertaking did not provide a service.

Whether there would be any functions left for the Traffic Commissioners in dealing with passenger traffic after the original transport areas were drawn up is debatable. The boundaries of areas might need to be altered from time to time but this would only be an occasional function. The simplest procedure as far as small rural operators were concerned might be to allow them to operate services wherever the major undertaking did not function, though this would involve finding some formula to deal with the situation where routes overlapped. A minimum percentage of any route operated by a small independent undertaking would have to be off the main undertaking's route. This would create some problems for the Traffic Commissioners or other licensing authority.

There would be no real need for the organization of the suggested transport 'boards,' as they may be called to distinguish them from existing undertakings, to be uniform throughout the country. A modified public corporation form of administration would seem to be most appropriate. A small board (varying with the size and population of the area served, which might be much larger for a board centred on Manchester or Birmingham than for one based on Leicester) of full-time members would be desirable. Neither the local authority committee of part-time and changing councillors, nor the company system of directors who, like those of Midland Red, have interests in important and completely different business activities seem particularly suitable for a board which would need to deal with the complicated, difficult and rapidly changing problems of passenger transport in Britain. A majority of the board should be appointed by the Minister of Transport and one or two chosen from the nominees of the appropriate local authorities. In some areas the new boards could be formed from a reorganization of existing Transport Holding Company undertakings. The boards would compete in so far as their performances in building up public road transport and in meeting whatever financial obligations were laid upon them could be compared. The present control over fares by the Transport Commissioners would cease to have any purpose and could be ended. It seems unlikely that a private equity holding in the boards would be desirable.

If government policy is to aim at bringing about a redistribution of passenger traffic between cars and buses some criterion for choosing between roads or areas where a car-to-bus transfer is desirable and those where it is not, is required. It is important that it would be clear to those involved that government action results in most of them being better off. It would, for example, be very difficult to gain popular acceptance for a congestion tax where the theoretical gains accrue to the whole community rather than to road users, and where even those road users continuing to use their cars would be worse off in that, although travelling more quickly, they would have to pay a tax high enough to reduce the size of their consumers surplus. The most straightforward and generally acceptable criterion for a car-to-bus transfer brought about by government action would be to show that the average door-to-door journey time of travellers would be reduced. Of all the various methods of bringing about a greater use of buses, the choice in the short run seems to lie between giving the buses some kind of priority on the roads, imposing a congestion tax, and the use of parking controls. A planned control of parking seems to present the fewest problems though it would entail legislation to extend public control over private parking spaces. The pricing mechanism could be used to allocate parking spaces, with some safeguards. It might be possible to devise a system whereby information about the availability of city centre parking space was shown on signs on main approaches to the city, where a switch to public transport was still possible.

The railways are still not actively seeking commuter traffic in most areas, and in Leicester seem to be resigned to their present position of making an insignificant contribution to the carriage of people to work. National transport policy should allow for the increased use of rail by commuter traffic even if this cannot be carried profitably. Indeed profit maximization, or loss minimization, may be a bad guide to what is in the long-term national interest in relation to rail passenger traffic. The most profitable passenger traffic for rail, which they have been seeking assiduously in recent years, is the carriage of long distance passengers on trunk routes. But with the development of motorways this is the kind of traffic which road coaches can carry as quickly and considerably more cheaply, than rail. It is at least probable that if all the costs and benefits were calculated, a much stronger case could have been made out for capital expenditure on improving rail commuter services in the large cities than on electrifying the London–Birmingham–Manchester line. (It may equally well be true that if all the sums had been done it would have been shown that the money should have been spent on the roads and not on the railways at all.) Inter-urban trunk roads and motorways are being improved and extended and will eventually be able to carry all long distance rail passenger traffic (except for a few roads at holiday peaks) without being overloaded. But as has already been argued there is no prospect that urban roads will be adequate for all the traffic seeking to use them at least for the rest of this century. The same line of argument also leads to the conclusion that it may be more important, in the national interest, for the railways to carry a bigger share of commuter traffic than it is for them to regain goods traffic from road vehicles. The railways are not an end in themselves and there is not necessarily any gain to the community because they capture long distance passenger traffic from air lines or manage to prevent the increased use of express coach services. But for the foreseeable future it will be in the national interest if they can carry more commuters to work in the large cities.

There are many topics relating to urban passenger transport which require much more detailed study than has been possible in this survey. These include methods of reducing the severity of peak demand; the applicability of the transfer criterion of shorter average journey time to actual roads and areas; studies of parking and the machinery by which it might be controlled; the justification for below-cost transport in rural areas; the possible development of rail commuter services; and the importance of journey time as a factor influencing travellers' choice of transport mode. The problems of urban passenger transport can be met only by many partial solutions, not by any single panacea, and the selection of the solutions which will work, rather than those which will not, can only be made by careful investigation of the realities of the ways in which people can be moved from place to place in the towns of today.

INDEX

INDEX

INDEX

INDEX

INDEX